Sessions

SESSIONS

A Self-Help Guide through Psychotherapy

by
Ann Patterson Wildemann, Ph.D.

A Crossroad Book
The Crossroad Publishing Company
New York

1996
The Crossroad Publishing Company
370 Lexington Avenue, New York, NY 10017

Copyright © 1996 by Ann Patterson Wildemann

Printed in the United States of America

Library of Congress Cataloging-in-Publication Data

Wildemann, Ann Patterson.
    Sessions : a self-help guide through psychotherapy / by Ann
Patterson Wildemann.
        p.   cm.
    Includes bibliographical references.
    ISBN 0-8245-1559-5 (pbk.)
    1. Change (Psychology).   2. Peace of mind.   3. Healing—Religious
aspects—Christianity.   4. Self-help techniques.   5. Counseling.
6. Psychotherapy—Popular works.   I. Title.
BF637.C4W55   1996
158'.1—dc20   95-51291
                                                                      CIP

In memory of my beloved Dad

Contents

Sessions

Session 1: The Process of Healing

Issues we will cover in Session 1:

- **Explaining the therapeutic process** — Therapy can be your opportunity to achieve any psychological or physical goal you choose.
- **Seven basic principles** — These are my beliefs about therapy as a process for change.
- **Free will and responsibility** — You are free to choose . . . but let's discuss the consequences of choice.
- **Introspection** — Peace and healing begin with introspection.
- **Meaning** — Illness or problems often provide "benefits" in disguise, so we need to look at exogains.

Session 2: Your Beliefs

Issues we will cover in Session 2:

- **Windows** — Our needs give us a window into our pathology.
- **Values in conflict** — Despair is often the result of not knowing what you value, and mental illness and stress are the by-products of values in conflict.
- **Permissions** — Rules say what you can and cannot do, and you define these rules yourself based on your values.
- **Life structures** — The rules you have built structure your beliefs about yourself.
- **Change** — Getting healthy means changing your belief system by introducing doubt into that system.

Session 3: Looking at You

Issues we will cover in Session 3:

- **Self-concept** — How we view ourselves is based on many factors, but its significance is that we behave according to this view.
- **Toxicity** — Sometimes we incorporate the negative things people say about us and surrender our power in the process.
- **Turning points** — Life changing events that impact your self-concept can be as simple as an off-handed remark or as major as a significant milestone.
- **Love** — Loving yourself is essential to health and growth.

Session 4: Your Beginnings

Issues we will cover in Session 4:

- **Intrafamilial dynamics** — We'll look at your family patterns and how they have influenced you.
- **Genogram** — This is a family tree that lets you take a unique look at you.
- **Making changes** — You cannot change anyone but yourself.

Session 5: Moving from the Pain

Issues we will cover in Session 5:

- **Linear regression** — Access your past.
- **Dysfunctional families** — They're all alike in one way or another and display a pattern of similar beliefs and laws.
- **Hiding secrets** — Troubled families live by certain laws.
- **By-products** — Laws are the behavioral by-product of family laws and include roles of discipline, confusion, and abuse.
- **Enabling personal growth** — You are the only person who can make the decision to live, not just exist.

Session 6: Mind–Body

Issues we will cover in Session 6:

- **Nexus of mind and body** — This connection can't be broken, and becoming aware of this fact is your path to well being.
- **Necessity for love, maintaining hope, and finding meaning in life** — We literally can't live without these important expressions of our human nature.
- **Will, the action part of hope** — Will is the verb that empowers hope.
- **Abuse and illness** — You may be suffering from this legacy of dysfunction and pain, which is the underpinning of many psychological and physical disorders.
- **The Environment** — I will help you make your physical environment a haven and fill your emotional environment with good relationships.
- **Implications of stress** — Stress has a definite impact on illness.

Session 7: The Self under Stress

Issues we will cover in Session 7:

- **Stress** — Stress is not just disease inducing, it's also vital for healthy motivation.
- **Effects of personality on stress** — We all deal with stress differently, but by identifying the personality styles of yourself and others, you can minimize the impact of stress.
- **De-stressors** — I'll give you some tools you can begin using immediately.
- **Interpretation Loop** — By understanding this loop and combining it with the Accuracy Mechanism and Choice Mechanism, communication as well as decision making become easy: $P\text{-}E\text{-}I = (P_R \, B_R) + (AM + CM) = P!$

Session 8: Defense

Issues we will cover in Session 8:

- **Skewed needs** — Intrusions from our past, left unsettled, can program you for destructive behaviors and illness.

- **Defense mechanisms** — In troubled families you learn ways to protect yourself.
- **Poisonous voices** — Your head may be filled with fears generated by this cancerous internal voice, which you can combat by "reframing" with the truth.
- **Four fears** — The four major categories of fear are rejection, anger, trauma, and failure (or success), and at least one or more of these may be keeping you in bondage.
- **Reparenting** — Learn how fear relates to old beliefs, events, goals, and old truths, and change them into new truths and new results.

Session 9: Shame, Guilt, and Self-Sabotage

Issues we will cover in Session 9:

- **Love as conditional or unconditional** — The quality of love experienced in childhood can create a lifetime of trouble.
- **Shame and guilt** — These feelings are hidden behind emotional illness.
- **Addictions, abuse, and conditional love** — These dysfunctions create shame-based people.
- **Detoxification** — You have the power to detoxify your shame.
- **Boundaries** — Have you been allowed to develop healthy boundaries or forced to build desperate bunkers?

Session 10: Therapy from the Soul

Issues we will cover in Session 10:

- **Therapy from the soul** — Art, dreams, meditation, prayer.
- **Guardian angels** — This spirit is within you.
- **The child spirit** — This concept is not "hokey" after all and, as a special part of the self, may just provide a direct pipeline to your emotional health.
- **The keeper of pain** — The child within you is burdened with all the pain and abuse accumulated from your past.
- **Reparenting** — These exercises can help you experience the unconditional love you missed.
- **Kelly's story** — Kelly's child spirit saved her life.
- **Metaphors for life** — These word tools help you see yourself differently.

Session 11: Anger

Issues we will discuss in Session 11:

- **Destructive anger** — As the result of painful childhoods, some people learn to turn anger against themselves while others externalize anger and violate those around them.
- **Physiological changes** — Effects of anger can be physical with symptoms that can actually be measured.
- **Biological rage** — Alzheimer's disease, Huntington's chorea, tumors, head injuries, birth injuries, convulsions are only some of the possible causes of rage suffered by some people.
- **Anger patterns** — Most of us fall within specific patterns of behavior in regard to the way we deal with or exhibit anger.
- **Self-anger** — Self-sabotaging behavior is often about being angry at yourself.
- **Appropriate confrontation** — Learn how to confront those who make you angry and turn anger into something constructive.
- **Empowerment** — Primal screaming, mattress work, breathing techniques.

Session 12: Forgiveness

Issues we will discuss in Session 12:

- **Being unforgiving** — When we are unable to forgive, the costs are too high in personal failures.
- **Faith** — The foundation of our very existence and our ability to forgive is faith, which is a belief in God or a higher power.
- **Charity** — Only when we express and extend our hearts may we feel forgiven.
- **Grace** — Forgiveness is helped by grace, which represents God's total unconditional love for us.
- **Self-forgiveness** — Being able to forgive others is impossible without being able to forgive yourself first.
- **Forgiving others** — Perpetually carrying around terrible memories is heavy baggage that impedes the process of forgiveness.
- **Heal yourself** — Steps to self-forgiveness enable you to replace old painful memories with fresh positive ones.

Introduction

Cancer of the Soul

After years of counseling with patients, I have begun to think that emotional problems are like "cancers of the soul." Cancer manifests itself through out-of-control growth, spreading into and incapacitating physiological functioning. Similarly, emotional illness incapacitates the soul. Like cancer, emotional problems begin in an early, silent, almost undetectable stage, separating us from love, the bread of life. As a problem worsens or spreads, it begins to affect other areas of the patient's life. Just as cancer in some cases leads to death, cancer of the soul can sometimes lead to total social withdrawal or even to suicide.

When I read through the descriptions of emotional dysfunction in the *Diagnostic and Statistical Manual of Mental Disorders*[1] (a reference book used by mental health professionals and developed by psychiatrists to catalogue and describe mental illnesses, covering subjects from anxiety to schizophrenia), the common message among all of these disorders is that something is out of control that is compromising patients' healthy abilities and causing them pain. This limit of good will destroys the natural response to ward off enemies within.

If you are struggling with old scars and pain from childhood and unmet needs in adulthood, you may be finding it difficult to make it through another day, another week, another month. Disappointments in relationships and in life events cloud our perceptions and intensify our feelings of self-doubt, guilt, fear, and anger. These toxic feelings modify our judgment and greatly compromise our chances for success and happiness. Frustrations and seemingly insurmountable challenges multiply.

Many people move from one crisis to another feeling unfulfilled and depressed, enjoying little about their lives. These are all good people, but they suffer from headaches, anxiety, muscle tension, and low self-esteem—their shoulders are burdened with problems. Unhappiness takes many forms; so, looking for relief, some turn to alcohol, chronic illnesses, drugs, inappropriate relationships, and other forms of disease to ease their pain.

In the following "sessions," I take the role of a silent doctor, guiding you along the road to resolutions and recovery. I believe that each day brings with it new opportunities for healing and healthy growth. Taking a critical look at ourselves (and truly being honest) is a test of maturity. It is not easy to accept that you have problems, pain, and shame. By looking at those issues, you can release your pain, deal with it, and move forward toward a better life. Although we don't wield a scalpel in psychotherapy, someone once said that therapy is sometimes like having surgery without the benefit of an anesthetic. *Sessions* takes a more gentle approach because it is influenced by the spiritual aspect of humanity.

I believe more than anything that we are our own co-creators. We share a personal and creative partnership with God in our physical, as well as spiritual, being. In my mind, I see my creator as a loving parent, cheering me on when times are good and providing unconditional support when times are difficult. We are free to make choices, for better or worse, in a life that presents us with all the challenges to chart our own course.

Does everybody solve everything while in therapy? It depends on the passion and desire for change, but an overwhelming number of people who go through therapy do improve their lives and find peace. They stop their aberrant cycles, and they begin to understand what motivates their behavior, and that, in turn, enables them to break the recurrence of destructive patterns.

What about you and the reason that has brought you to read this book? If the opposite of love is fear, are you ready to face your fear and accept the present challenge? If you are, then I am eager to begin this special journey with you. A word of caution, however: Please complete the written exercises as they arise in the reading. If you don't work, neither does this book. If you were totally happy with life, you would not have come this far in your reading, so please be true to yourself. Work along with me—and begin realizing your own miracles!

Let's begin . . .

Discovery

The Process of Healing

Issues we will cover in Session 1:

- **Explaining the therapeutic process** — Therapy can be your opportunity to achieve any psychological or physical goal you choose.
- **Seven basic principles** — These are my beliefs about therapy as a process for change.
- **Free will and responsibility** — You are free to choose . . . but let's discuss the consequences of choice.
- **Introspection** — Peace and healing begin with introspection.
- **Meaning** — Illness or problems often provide "benefits" in disguise, so we need to look at exogains.

As you enter my office, you will notice colors of nature—mauves, greens, purples, and gold . . .

You will find a very comfortable sofa with many pillows on it and a matching love seat. There are two large, high-backed, deep-green chairs, one of which I use. Almost all of my patients prefer to sit on the sofa. The room contains many windows, books, plants, and pictures, some of which are of my children. At the far end of the room sits a large desk with two chairs in front of it. I use the desk only for paperwork. My patients tell me that my office is like being in a warm home—an atmosphere of healing and acceptance—and that is just the impression I want my work environment to convey.

I want you to get into a nice, comfortable position and try to let your mind and body relax. If you have never gone through therapy, you are in for a wonderful experience. You will inevitably experience some pain along the way, but, just as surely, you will grow, overcoming old traumas as you seek healing. You will gain strength at each juncture. If this is not your first experience with therapy, you will have the opportunity to go over areas in which you have not completed the healing process in order finally to resolve those old issues.

I will begin by telling you how I view the therapeutic process . . .

I believe that therapy is an intellectual and deeply spiritual process by which you can overcome fears, sadness, pain, and anxiety by using your mind as the most important therapeutic tool at your disposal. This process can be greatly enhanced by working with a therapist who offers guidance through feedback and interpretation. With this help I believe you can achieve any psychological goal you choose. For example, many of my patients elect to work on emotional wellness issues, the most important of which is healing. They may decide to free themselves at last from painful childhood memories such as abuse issues that have left them with a sense of powerlessness and caused them to feel worthless and shameful. Still others may have a less-heavy agenda and may set as their goal the elimination of self-sabotaging behaviors that have kept them from the success and happiness they wish. Whatever your goal, now is the time to establish it as we begin our sojourn.

Statement of your therapeutic goal . . .

Ask yourself: Why have I come to counseling? What is my pain? The following are examples of patients' responses:

- I want to help myself by using my mind and soul to heal my emotional pain.
- I want to stop my fears and overcome my traumatic childhood.
- I want to find out why I am so unhappy.
- I want to stop feeling so empty and confused.

Please write out the reasons you're here and—this is important—read them out loud to yourself.

Your mind is your tool . . .

With your goal now firmly in mind, let me continue telling about my beliefs concerning psychotherapy. I believe that our creator has endowed us with the most marvelous and miraculous tool of all creation, the human mind. And I believe this was done so that we could practice free will, be autonomous, and put this gift to work to bring about power from within and from without. I must emphasize that I feel that life is for loving and living, not suffering and dying. I also believe that we are each here for a purpose, and part of getting well and achieving that healing, overcoming those childhood traumas, or finding happiness is predicated on identifying our own unique meaning and experience and being open to change our perceptions. Along the way we need to respect always each individual and to recognize that each of us has a unique purpose in life.

Much of mental illness stems from difficult childhoods, lack of direction, poor choices, and unmet needs, as well as conflict in values and beliefs. People become so bogged down in life's daily demands and personal struggles that they lose sight of the broader questions that ask: Why are we here? How do you know what you are meant to do? I hope that by the end of this book you will have begun to answer these questions. I want to put forth the suggestion that each of us is capable of discovering our purpose. I also am convinced that "cancers of the soul" are trying to teach us individually something about our life and our reason for being here.

When I began the difficult task of putting my beliefs into writing, beliefs influenced by what all my patients have taught me, I conceptualized some simple premises that act as a specific foundation for therapy.

Seven Basic Principles

1. Every person has been endowed with free will.
2. Everyone is responsible for his or her actions.
3. Peace and healing begin with introspection.
4. Introspection necessitates listening to your soul.
5. Gaining peace and healing is a process that can be learned and taught.
6. This process produces miracles.
7. Miracles produce love, which is a gift that brings meaning and healing.

The first of these premises is . . .

1. Every person has been endowed with free will.

We have the right as human beings to make decisions, good or bad, right or wrong, even when we feel that our choices are negative. Ultimately, we still have the right to choose. There is no such thing as "I had no choice." This free will stuff, however, sometimes becomes clouded by self-lies and excuses, which ultimately become obstacles we must overcome. Emerging from the darkness is a choice.

A companion to free will and choice is responsibility. Thus, my next premise . . .

2. Everyone is responsible for his or her actions.

When we decide to put our pleasure before our obligations, we must take responsibility for that choice. Why is it that so many people avoid taking responsibility? Possibly because accepting responsibility often involves pain, and it does so in two ways.

First, if I am responsible for my actions, then I must accept the consequences, good or bad. I cannot, for example, say, "I am not to blame for my behavior because my boss is unfair." Or, "My spouse is the reason I drink." Excuses cause more pain and prevent happiness and growth.

The second way that pain arises out of taking responsibility is that I can no longer dwell on the past and use it as a crutch. In essence that is what an excuse is—merely a crutch. While many of my patients indeed experienced abominable childhoods, there comes a time when they must say, "Yes, I was unjustly treated and abused. It clearly was not my fault that my parents mistreated me, but now I must face that it occurred in my past and, while it helps to explain why I do the things I do, I am now responsible for my behavior." This insight is the cornerstone for your mental health and healing, along with miracles that help align your perceptions with truth as God created it.

It is hard to let go of old pains and hurts, but it is important to begin letting go of the past and not let it nag at you or allow yourself to indulge in self-pity or pity from others. You are worth far more than pity. You have the courage to make the necessary changes to achieve your goals.

My next premise is . . .

3. Peace and healing begin with introspection.

In order to see out, one first must see in. In order to understand life and others, we must first understand ourselves. The only way to accomplish peace and healing is to look carefully inside and discover the kind of person we really are—to answer "Who am I?" Through introspection one begins to tap into the unconscious, the keeper of the secrets and memories, the place that silently influences our behavior.

What is it like to be me? This is quite a provocative question, and it needs to be answered. I now would like you to write out the answer to that question by considering the following.

Define yourself in God's terms . . .

What is it like to be me?

How do I feel about my ability to love, to be happy, to be successful?

What are the two most important issues in my life?

1.

2.

Who loves me?

Whom do I love?

How do I feel about my work?

What is my home life like?

How do I feel about a greater, or spiritual, power?

How would I describe how God sees me?

You will need some time to complete these answers. Do it slowly and carefully. Keep your goal in mind, and remember that through your pain and illness, you can allow that "cancer of the soul" to change your life for the better. One grows through love. If pain is in your life, however, you have the opportunity to use it to find that love.

This business of getting in touch with ourselves requires looking into where we really live—tapping into the soul. God is about love, not pain.

4. Introspection necessitates listening to your soul.

Every disease, illness, or problem carries with it something we call exogains. In other words, we have long known in psychiatry that each illness acts out a benefit in disguise. For example, I often see homemakers who suddenly develop migraines or other psychogenic illnesses after their children have left the nest and gone off to college or into the world. All of a sudden these dedicated moms have their role taken away, causing them to feel unneeded. This is especially true of women who centered their lives around their children and whose husbands have emotionally gone their own way. Now there is only pain left. Do they want the pain? No, but the pain does create a purpose in its demand for attention, which they desperately need because of their often emotionally remote husbands and their absent children. The pain may also provide them with something to do—going to the doctor—and gives them something to talk about. Is this done on a conscious level? Again, no. I work with this wife and mother and help her to redirect her energies and feel needed again; she takes responsibility for her pain and is able to work through it. She steps into the light by developing self-love. She learns that pain and love cannot coexist.

Perhaps your illness may be of a more severe nature such as depression with thoughts of suicide, or other life-threatening disorders such as alcoholism or drug abuse. Looking within is imperative. You do this by asking yourself . . . more questions. The first is, as with our homemaker, What purpose does my illness serve? This is certainly not to imply that you have the disease because you want attention or that the disease is your fault, but with every disorder there is some self-punishment and payoff involved. What you get from your disease is often what you feel you deserve. If you become ill, look at your family life—are you escaping through illness? Look at your job—is it literally making you sick? What about relationships? Start making some changes because life is too short to spend it in suffering. Write out your answers to these questions:

1. What purpose does my illness or problem serve?
2. What am I escaping?
3. What is the relationship of my job to my illness or problem?
4. How does my illness or problem affect the people I love?

Finding meaning in your illness or pain . . .

We spoke earlier about meaning, and I mentioned the importance of finding meaning in your life, but before you can do this, you must first find meaning in your illness, problems, or unhappiness. You are the work of God, and God's work is wholly loving. Talk to your illness by thoughtfully and carefully answering the above questions and find out how depression, obsessions, compulsive and destructive behaviors, or failures are serving you. What feelings are engendered in you as a result of these problems? Do you need to forgive yourself for past behavior in order to be free from your affliction?

Sometimes reflecting back prior to your illness or problem—perhaps six months to two years—can give you some answers. Did you suffer a loss through death, divorce, employment, career, relationship? Sometimes these happenings become a trigger in the body and mind, setting the stage for mental or physical illness. Use the following time line to look at the two years before you became depressed or began having physical or emotional problems, and write what happened to you during those periods of time to help you answer the preceding questions

2 months before my depression or illness:

6 months before:

12 months before:

18 months before:

24 months before:

Remember to think in terms of occurrences—good or bad—that happened during these periods. People sometimes can't experience a truly happy event because they feel their "deserve level" is so low. Not only can they not enjoy it, but the happiness itself may cause or trigger problems. We will be looking more closely at your self-concept and deserve level, but for now, just fill in this time line. (Sometimes it is helpful to ask a loved one to jog your memory.)

It is not unusual for me to see a patient who apparently is doing well but can't seem to shake anxiety and fear of impending doom. Often when we look back over this patient's recent life events, he or she may have insufficiently grieved over the death of a parent or loved one, and now, several years later, this patient is having symptoms of sleeplessness, despair, emptiness, problems with concentration, and memory loss. Anxiety disorders and panic disorders are rooted in the past, sometimes in the near past. By discovering the origin of these disorders, the patient is able to find relief.

What we have been doing together relates to my next two premises . . .

5. Gaining peace and healing is a process that can be learned and taught.

Gaining peace and healing does seem to require some specific steps. First of all, I think it is reasonable to decide that thus far you have been calling all of the shots, and as you have discovered, much to your chagrin, things are not going well. You may have achieved power, money, prestige, and possessions, yet you feel angry, unhappy, despairing, disappointed, and sick. Or perhaps you experience some of these same emotions but feel that you have not accomplished much. You may be unemployed, burdened by financial worries, or feel you have missed achieving the American dream.

Many of us have a "need" to control, but this aberrant need often is the source of our undoing. This control issue ultimately leads to being out of control as expressed by emotional pains, nervous breakdowns, and physical illness. There is a better way, and taking that first step, recognizing we need some help, begins the process.

This next step involves a willingness to allow for a shift in our perception of things. When we are willing to challenge our perceptions—the way we see things—then a miracle occurs. For example, if you believe that God or a higher power created or made possible everything we see, then it follows that God is in everything we see. Searching for God in an event, a person, or an illness that causes us pain puts us in touch with love, and thus a shift in our perception occurs. So does a miracle. It is virtually impossible not to feel love when you see God.

Emotional and physical illnesses are wake-up calls that give us an opportunity to change our business-as-usual attitudes. The second step is inviting the Holy Spirit into our lives, letting in the light. Choosing to let love into your life quietly sets the stage for peace and healing. I do not believe that calling upon the Holy Spirit involves much fanfare or formality. Simply a sincere and prayerful request—"Holy Spirit, please help me"— is enough.

6. This process produces miracles.

You were born with five senses for your survival, but I believe that introspection may be a sixth sense, and that is the one you have just been using! This introspection and therapy from the soul will be your healer. It will allow you to create miracles. A miracle is merely an expression of love. Disease is the absence of self-love, which creates a sense of lack. Patients express this sense of lack by such comments as "not feeling well enough," "less than up to par," "not up to snuff," "no energy," or "too weak." When you practice self-love, you honor what God has created. You begin to love, and this dissipates any feelings of separation from God manifested through a sense of isolation and deprivation. Patients will tell me that they feel alone, misunderstood, and confused, that they lack a sense of connection and belonging. Someone once said that if you feel that you are far from God, . . . guess who moved?

And so the last premise is . . .

7. Miracles produce love, which is a gift that brings meaning and healing.

Just as my patients have benefited from this process of working through illness and personal problems, so can you. God wants us to be happy and to share our joy with others. With every step in that direction we come closer to love.

How ready are you to let the healing light in—to be able to achieve all of your goals? It's time to find out. Below you will find a simple matrix that will let you know these answers. All that you need to do is answer yes or no and then total up your responses.

Motivation	Dedication	Plan	Total
Do you want to change?	Will you read the book?	Specific time for reading.	_____ (1–3)
Are you unhappy with life as it is?	Will you do the exercises?	Specific time for writing.	_____ (1–3)
Is your pain intolerable?	Will you review your progress?	Specific time for review.	_____ (1–3)
Can you be good to you?	Will you make you a priority?	Specific time for meditation.	_____ (1–3)
			_____ (4–12)

A total of 6 or more = Yes, you are ready!

The columns that I have labeled embrace three important words—motivation, dedication, and plan. Whenever you want to accomplish a goal, those three critical elements must be employed. You may be saying, "But I am lazy so therefore I lack motivation." Please don't confuse laziness with lack of motivation. If you were lazy, you would not be this far into the book. If you weren't motivated, you would not have begun the book in the first place. The second word is dedication. Now that we are over the motivation hump, dedication is merely the way you manage your motivation. Undedicated folks would not have filled out the matrix. The last word is plan. A plan simply puts your motivation and dedication into action. Now add up your *yes* responses. If you have six or more, you are on your way to health—mentally, physically, and spiritually.

As you let this light in, you begin to move from your fears to love. You become more capable of searching from within. The ability to trust and climb begins.

Seven Basic Principles

1. Every person has been endowed with free will.
2. Everyone is responsible for his or her actions.
3. Peace and healing begin with introspection.
4. Introspection necessitates listening to your soul.
5. Gaining peace and healing is a process that can be learned and taught.
6. This process produces miracles.
7. Miracles produce love, which is a gift that brings meaning and healing.

Your Beliefs

Issues we will cover in Session 2:

- **Windows** — Our needs give us a window into our pathology.
- **Values in conflict** — Despair is often the result of not knowing what you value, and mental illness and stress are the by-products of values in conflict.
- **Permissions** — Rules say what you can and cannot do, and you define these rules yourself based on your values.
- **Life structures** — The rules you have built structure your beliefs about yourself.
- **Change** — Getting healthy means changing your belief system by introducing doubt into that system.

In our last session you took the first step in the process of therapy . . .

Let's look at what you have accomplished thus far. You identified your goals in therapy—the results that you want to attain. Next, you began to define yourself through a very personal inventory. Then you took a very painful, but enlightening, assessment of the purpose your illness serves. By reflecting back two years before the onset of your symptoms, you may have discovered a trigger or precipitating event. And finally, you considered your readiness to change.

Before proceeding, please go back and review your answers to the exercises in Session 1. As we move through each session, I will ask you to reread the work you've done. This ongoing review will act as an important framework for your therapy. Very shortly, you will be experiencing what I call the "Ah ha!" phenomenon—various insights will begin to come together to help explain what has happened to you and why. This is the gateway to change.

I know that it takes courage to face fear and to stay committed. In this session we are going to take a closer look at you and the special, unique person that you are. First, we will talk about needs, the basics of life. Our needs give us a window to see into our pathology. Most folks carry out their daily tasks around their needs, either avoiding situations that are painful or indulging in situations that bring pleasure.

Next, we will look at your *values, rules,* and *beliefs.* How were your beliefs developed, and of those beliefs, which ones are serving you poorly and causing damage? Along with this identification of beliefs, we will look at how you can change these systems to make life happier, because our beliefs become rules that are based on values. Tapping into these three areas answers many questions about why your life is not as fulfilling as it can be. You are moving on in the therapeutic process. Growth can hurt, but not if you keep in mind to seek the love.

Let's discuss satisfaction of needs . . .

One of the most important prerequisites for change and growth is understanding and satisfying your needs. Many years ago a researcher by the name of Abraham Maslow[2] described our needs as being related to our development as individuals. He used a hierarchical configuration to help demonstrate what he meant:

Physiological — air, food, water
Safety — shelter, clothing, secure environment
Love and Belonging — being loved, loving family
Esteem and Recognition — feeling appreciated, respected, good
Cognitive — acquiring knowledge, satisfying curiosity, understanding
Aesthetic — enhancing life with art, beauty, order, and structure
Self-Actualization — reaching one's potential, full self-expression

Physiological needs are life's basic requirements for air, food, and water. These basic needs are the underpinnings of survival and the first to be satisfied in order to sustain life. A newborn upon delivery cries out and expands its lungs to take in the first gulp of oxygen. The baby continues to cry and is placed at the mother's breast to enable the infant to take in milk.

If those initial needs of food and oxygen are not met, the result is death. If these needs are satisfied, however, the next level, which he calls Safety, becomes dominant.

Safety includes having shelter, clothing, and an environment out of harm's way. What happens, however, if your mother and father did not protect you from others or, worse, what if they were the abusers? The consequence is a betrayal of trust—the very foundation of mental health. This breach in trust leads to a legacy of fears often manifested by "cancers of the soul." So how is it that children manage to survive this level?

I believe that we each are fortified by love and that love is an integral part of our deep psyche. It is that love that survives the abuses of this stage. Sustained abuse, however, gives rise to illnesses (mental and physical). At early and vulnerable ages, we are unsure or ignorant about how to reach that God-given love within us, the products of the soul, to use in our defense. We then are fearful and become ill. The illness becomes a defense in our desperate efforts to protect ourselves against abuse. The insight we can gain from this reality is just another way to express fear and the consequences of not being safe. Fear is without; love is within.

If you do feel safe, though, then you can move to higher-level needs, the next being **Love and Belonging.** This level includes feeling nurtured, and this allows you to love in return, feeling a part of a family and having friends, experiencing unity and bonding.

If we were to look at mental and emotional illness and health on a continuum and insert Maslow's levels, this is how I think these concepts would look:

[————General Range of Problems————]

Level 1	Level 2	Level 3	Level 4	Level 5	Level 6	Level 7
Death	Psychosis	[————Neuroses————]				
Physio-logical	→ Safety	→ Love and Belonging	→ Esteem and Recognition	→ Cognitive	→Aesthetic	→ Self-Actualization

This chart attempts to show that mental problems (or even death) are likely if certain needs are not met at each stage. Also, the theory shows that transcending or moving from stage to stage becomes progressively harder and perhaps impossible to achieve if the needs of the stage that came before are not met. Although the above chart represents a gradual progression (or failure) to achieve each level of the seven stages of human needs, I think Maslow's scheme is more complicated than that. I like to interpret his model as showing that the needs of all stages are present in all of us at every age, but the levels become, in turn, consciously out front or subconsciously buried depending on individual life situations. As Maslow intended, it is a simple hierarchical picture of one's lifetime needs from birth to death, but this process can also represent an overlapping, interrelated, and continuous process of meeting, or failing to meet, these specific needs in the face of each new experience that may occur in your life.

I believe that people can acquire and maintain an acceptable level of mental health—and even achieve the Aesthetic Stage 6 and the Self-Actualizing Stage 7—even though abuse or neglect has occurred in all or some of the stages. I think it is possible in all cases, but it depends on how each person manages to get those needs met. It is not what happened to us so much as what we do about it. For that matter, we all probably experience at least some sort of abuse or neglect at every stage, whether the abuse comes from parents or other significant people in our lives or is inflicted on us just by the impersonal cultural expectations of society in general! Society is devoid of the spirit of community.

At the third level we are still working with fairly simple needs, but in the next level, which is called **Esteem and Recognition,** we are merging into an area where a human becomes a more noble entity and can begin functioning, psychologically and spiritually, in a healthy arena. This is the highest level most people will reach, but it is a level at which people can live a happy and productive life. All of the previous levels of needs have been met. To become optimally fulfilled, however, the final level must be achieved—the level of Self-Actualization, unconditional love.

Self-actualizers are people who have fully developed their talents and skills and who often are humanitarians, such as Albert Schweitzer and Mother Teresa of Calcutta, or researchers such as John Watson or Albert Einstein. But I also believe that there are plenty of common people who are self-actualized, including truck drivers and ministers and housewives and teachers and students and politicians and nurses and accountants.

The higher-level needs—**Cognitive, Aesthetic,** and **Self-Actualization** — are the most difficult to achieve. People who seek self-actualization have managed to fulfill their cognitive needs by exploring knowledge and understanding about life and themselves. They have taken a psychological and spiritual journey, just as you are doing! And they have achieved their aesthetic needs by striving to put beauty, order, and symmetry in their lives and relationships. Maslow is saying to us that in order to be really happy and productive, our needs for food, shelter, love, and esteem must first be met. Without rising satisfactorily through the basic steps, it is not possible to reach the personal fulfillment offered by the higher steps.

Many of my patients, even though they may have successful careers, tell me consistently that although they believe the first two levels of needs (Physiological and Safety) and, to some extent, even the third level (Love and Belonging) were met in childhood, they still suffer from low self-esteem. These feelings are the result of sad or abusive childhoods or come from some amount of neglect or total absence of their parents' love. With the help of therapy many begin to understand that this love was conditional, that in some way they had to earn it—love was not freely given. How can someone with this burden of suppressed feelings now be expected to be a wonderful parent or friend or spouse?

Someone once said that we nurture from our overflow . . .

That is, we give love, recognition, and understanding from the "extras" we already have. Again, these extras spring forth from needs that have been met and exceeded. If you are functioning from a state of lack, you are unable to give to others or to yourself. Sometimes people whose needs were not met appear either selfish or angry. Such people walk around feeling only emptiness and have the sense they are less than whole.

How can these people be helped? It is easier to state the answer than to cure the afflication. But, in the second half of the book we will do reparenting. Just as this sounds, we will go back to those painful areas and parent them appropriately this time—with love, kindness, and healing. In the meantime, take a look at Maslow's hierarchy of needs again and determine where you fit. At what level are you? Once you have looked at where you are, you can begin to establish some areas of your life to change, and you will be able to progress to where you want to be.

What needs do you have that are not being met? Please write out where you and your unmet needs are currently located. Even if you must begin at the level of Love and Belonging, that's fine. You are still okay, and you will still be able to heal those old wounds.

Now let's forge ahead and take a closer look at you . . .

I will do this by taking a history, which I hope you will find quite enlightening.

A Life-Script Questionnaire

Please write answers to the following questions:

1. List any physical problems you have.

2. What have you been told about your birth?

3. Describe your mother briefly as you remember her any time before you were twelve years old.

4. What would you have needed to do or say to please her when you were in the first, second, or third grade?

5. Describe your father briefly as you remember him any time before you were twelve years old.

6. What would you have needed to do or say to please him when you were in the first, second, or third grade?

7. What did your mother say when she complimented you (as early as you can remember)?

8. What did she say when she criticized you (as early as you can remember)?

9. How did she punish you? How did you feel when she did?

10. What did your father say when he complimented you?

11. What did he say when he criticized you (as early as you can remember)?

12. How did he punish you? How did you feel when he did?

13. What nicknames have people called you? What do the names mean to you?

14. What did your mother want you to be?

15. What do you do currently? Is it what you want to do?

16. What did your father want you to be?

17. What was your relationship to each brother or sister as you were growing up? Please state their names, differences in ages, and a short phrase about each to describe the relationship.

18. Describe your education and your employment history.

19. What is remarkable—either good or bad—about your high school, your college years, and the jobs you have held?

20. How do you express your angry feelings toward others?

21. Do you ever feel like something might be wrong with you? If yes, what?

22. Describe the bad feeling you have most often in your life. When did you first feel it?

23. What was the worst thing a parent or parent substitute ever did to you? How did you react?

24. If everything goes right, what will you be doing five years from today?

25. How do you think you will die? At what age?

26. How would you like to be remembered?

27. What would "heaven on earth" be for you?

28. What do you wish your mother had done differently in parenting you?

29. What do you wish your father had done differently in parenting you?

30. How are you as a parent?

31. If you could change anything about you by magic, what would you change?

32. Describe any other significant female in your life before the age of ten.

33. Describe any other significant male in your life before the age of ten.

34. How many marriages have you had? Please list and say what happened.

35. How many children do you have? List names, ages, and three characteristics.

36. Describe your current spouse or "significant other." Is your marriage or relationship satisfying? Are you happy?

37. What about your work or career? Are you where you thought you would be? What happens next?

Sometimes it is of great benefit not just to list the descriptions and events of your life script, but to put them into sentence and story form. You may use your answers as an outline from which to build your story and then make additional comments. Read your story out loud—first to yourself and then to a trusted family member or friend. Ask for their input. See what they might add.

One of your latest accomplishments is the development, through your answers to this questionnaire, of a life story...

Obviously, you have been doing a great deal of thinking while completing this questionnaire. Carefully look over these answers and pay close attention to patterns. For example, have you had more positive relationships with men or with women? We tend to marry or have relationships with people who are most like the parent with whom we had the most difficulty. So, if your wife reminds you of your mother, or your husband, your father, you now know where you need to do some work. Childhood memories are very important, so, overall, would you say they were more positive or negative?

If I seem to be focusing on your childhood rather than on the present, please don't become impatient. Out of our childhood we emerge to become productive and happy citizens, at least that is the goal. But if you are impaired by old wounds, your immediate need is to reduce the pain, and if you focus on alleviating pain, there is little time or energy left over for being happy. What we learn from the so-called truths about ourselves is often a direct throwback to childhood. One of the things I often say to my patients is that our parents are our first teachers. They teach us how to parent, how to raise a family, how to relate with spouses and significant others. And they teach us how to handle anger, develop belief systems, our moral code, and values. Childhood cannot be ignored!

A value differs from a rule or belief in that it is a standard or principle regarded as desirable or worthwhile . . .

Values are directly related to our self-image. Some common *values* that most of us hold would be honesty, love, freedom, courage, power, passion, health, spirituality, and a sense of family. In our contemporary life many would point to Lech Walensa as a man whose value of freedom turned him into a one-man army that helped to collapse communist Poland. His passion for freedom and his belief that it was achievable captured the imagination of the world and provided a precursor to the ultimate dismantling of suppression.

We all have values that we hold dear and to which we are fully committed. Part of the reason people find themselves in unhealthy situations that cause pain, indecisiveness, and despair, however, is that they don't know what they value. Some of this is the result of poor parenting, neglect, and abuse. If no one ever told you as a child that you possess greatness and that something deep inside could rise to achieve anything—including peace, happiness, and success—then now, as an adult, you are left with a self-defeating and perhaps miserable life.

Over and over I see patients who get up each morning dreading to go to their jobs, who come home to an unhappy marriage, have a drink, worry about tomorrow, watch TV, and go to bed—only to repeat this abysmal cycle the next day, day in and day out. Their *belief* is that life is a drudgery, and because their experience is familiar and one that they think they deserve, this belief helps keep them in their prisons. Does this sound familiar? They have accepted their existence based on their values, rules, and beliefs developed from childhood. Like it or not, all of our decisions stem from our values about life in general and about ourselves as individuals. If you were not valued as a child, chances are you won't value yourself as an adult.

In order to change your life you must first look at your values, rules, and beliefs and see what needs to be corrected. Write down a list of your values. Ask yourself, "What are the most important things I value?" Examples might be health, freedom, spirituality, money, love.

List eight values:	Arrange in order of most importance to you:
1.	
2.	
3.	
4.	
5.	
6.	
7.	
8.	

Knowing your values helps because:

- Values give direction to your life.
- Values allow you to understand why you make the choices you make, good or bad.

Now, from our values we develop rules—what we live by . . .

A *rule* is an authoritative statement based on a value that says what you can and cannot do. Some of the by-products of rules are guilt, conflict, self-sabotage, unhappiness, and depression. Not all rules are bad, indeed society counts on them to keep order and maintain a healthy populace. Examples of good rules are the following:

- Look both ways before you cross the street.
- Eat a balanced diet.
- Be kind to others.
- Obey the law.

The rules that are taught by dysfunctional families, however, result in maladaptive and compulsive behaviors. These patterns of behavior are defense mechanisms that are learned in order to cope with emotional trauma. Tragedy lies in the fact that these rules are passed from generation to generation unless there is intervention. Thus, lives are then structured around toxic rules. Some examples of inappropriate rules are the following:

- Don't cry.
- Get them before they get you.
- Always stick with your kind.
- Don't expect anything.

Perhaps you learned some rules about eating, alcohol and drugs, sickness, work, showing love and affection, sex, and family secrets. To demonstrate how these toxic values and rules work, let me give you some examples.

- Suppose the *value* was loyalty, so the companion *rule* is "Never tell family secrets." (On the surface this rule seems harmless—but what if the family secret is incest!) Your *belief* then would be "If I break the rule, I am disloyal and bad."
- If the *value* is love but the companion *rule* is "Always exhibit perfection," then your *belief* would be "If I am less than perfect, then I am not lovable or worthwhile."
- If the *value* is power, the *rule* might be "What I say, goes." The conflict is obvious. There is no room for discussion or compromise. The belief is "I am bad if I disobey. I am powerless."

What are your rules? Make your list of personal rules and be sure to cover (1) health, (2) love, (3) relationships, (4) work, (5) achievement,

(6) sex, (7) spirituality, (8) survival, (9) having fun, and (10) illness. Notice that I have included a column for beliefs. We will fill that in later.

RULES	BELIEFS
1. Health:	
2. Love:	
3. Relationship:	
4. Work:	
5. Achievement:	
6. Sex:	
7. Spirituality:	
8. Survival:	
9. Fun:	
10. Illness:	

The most fascinating aspect about rules, however, is that they set up our belief system . . .

Just as values give us direction, your rules can create happiness or sadness, good or bad feelings, success or failure. Rules structure our *beliefs* about how we feel about ourselves. Go back now to your list of personal rules and write the belief that is the result of each of your rules.

So, how can you tell if your rules are working against you? Ask yourself:

1. Is my rule impossible to meet?
2. Is my rule predicated on things beyond my control?
3. Does my rule allow for good feelings or bad feelings?

Go back over your rules applying your new questions to assess if your rules are working for you. Where do you need to make changes? For example:

RULE	BELIEF
If...your rule demands that in order to loved you must have undivided attention, must always feel secure, must always have total acceptance, must never have anger shown to you, and must always get along. . .	Then...your beliefs about your self-worth will be negative and painful.
If...your rule demands that in order to have fun on your vacation, the weather needs to be perfect. If the weather does not cooperate, you can't have any fun and will have wasted your time and money.	Then...your belief about yourself might be that nothing ever turns out right and that life is one disappointment after another. You would then say to yourself, "I always get cheated. I just always seem to have bad luck.
If...your rule sets you up to feel good or bad about yourself depending on whether people notice you or not.	Then...your belief tells you that you are often ignored or unfairly judged or that you are not appreciated.

The most hopeful aspect of all this is that anything learned can be unlearned—and that includes values, rules, and beliefs. To find the happiness and peace you desire, you must learn to understand your beliefs and make a conscious effort to change those that are damaging and belittling. In the process you will learn how to prevent others from robbing you of your health. Remember, a belief is a feeling of certainty about what something means. It becomes powerful because it is something that we just accept as fact and no longer question. The way to change negative beliefs is simply to introduce doubt. Ask the following questions:

• What if my belief is wrong?
• What evidence do I have that challenges that belief?
• What is the positive aspect to my belief?

So your values give you direction (up or down) and construct your rules (reasonable or unreasonable), and the rules establish your beliefs about yourself (negative or positive) . . .

We have just seen how important these three structures are to your self-image and, ultimately, your mental health. The interrelationship of your values, rules, and beliefs also affects your ability to meet the upper levels of Maslow's stages of needs.

Value		Rule		Belief		
+		+		+		
or	=	or	=	or	=	**Self-Image**
−		−		−		

Putting it all together . . .

Please go back to your hierachical list of eight values. Write a new rule you have made about each of those values and the positive belief it creates.

	Value	Rule	Belief
1.			
2.			
3.			
4.			
5.			
6.			
7.			
8.			
9.			
10.			

We have established together that all of these constructs are learned phenomena and are usually developed in those most important first two decades of life. They come together via our parents, teachers, peers, or authority figures—but that does not make them always correct!

Psychology teaches that our thoughts affect how we behave. When reviewing your values, rules, and beliefs, look for the love in these three categories. When there is conflict between your values and behaviors, what is achieved is illness. When we look at our belief system, claim it, and assume responsibility for the thoughts that created our system, a change can occur. Our behavior stems from that system, which again is based on our thoughts, so, to change a belief system, we must change our thoughts. If our values, rules, and beliefs are products of toxic thoughts, ask the Holy Spirit to step in and help us eliminate the old thoughts and create new healthy ones. You then will achieve what you believe!

Session 3 _____

Looking at You

_____

Issues we will cover in Session 3:

- **Self-concept** — How we view ourselves is based on many factors, but its significance is that we behave according to this view.
- **Toxicity** — Sometimes we incorporate the negative things people say about us and surrender our power in the process.
- **Turning points** — Life changing events that impact your self-concept can be as simple as an off-handed remark or as major as a significant milestone.
- **Love** — Loving yourself is essential to health and growth.

In Session 2 you accomplished some very introspective tasks. Using Maslow's Hierarchy-of-Needs list, you identified your needs that are not being met. You listed your values in order of importance, and you listed ten personal rules that you have developed from those values you've acquired. After considering how your rules affect the quality of your life, you were able to decide if your beliefs about yourself are negative or positive. Then you gained the insight that anything learned can be unlearned.

In this session we are now ready to take another step to tie things together and increase your discovery process . . .

We need to look at your self-concept, bringing with us the information you developed in Session 2 from your needs and your beliefs.

Our self-concept is the way in which we view ourselves. It is not what others think of us, although, as you have learned, that has a major impact. It is simply what we think of ourselves. (You will probably notice that from start to finish in our sessions together, we will be doing self-concept work.

Self-concept work is by no means limited to this session.) There are many components to the self-concept and here are several to get you started.

- On a scale of 1 to 5, 1 being the worst and 5 being the best, rate how you see yourself—and how you think others see you—on the chart below.
- Add up your score horizontally for each attribute.
- A score of less than 15 for each attribute means you need to do some work in that area.

HOW I SEE MYSELF

| | *How I see me* | | *How others see me* | | | |
	Me (1-5)	Spouse (1-5)	Children (1-5)	Parents (1-5)	Friends (1-5)	TOTALS
Attractiveness	_____	_____	_____	_____	_____	= _____
Intelligence	_____	_____	_____	_____	_____	= _____
Sense of Humor	_____	_____	_____	_____	_____	= _____
Emotionally	_____	_____	_____	_____	_____	= _____
Talents/Abilities	_____	_____	_____	_____	_____	= _____

Add the numbers in each horizontal line for a total for each attribute.

People sometimes confuse having a good self-concept with the negative connotations of self-love and conceit . . .

Even though some people think it is wrong to acknowledge nice things about themselves, they are mistaken. I hope you have 25s beside each attribute—but just in case you don't, we'll get it together later!

By now we have a pretty good picture of you and of how you and others see you. Because of childhood influences, you may find that your self-worth is low. If you are experiencing some anxiety or sadness, talk to a friend or to your family doctor. If this is too upsetting, you may want to stop, regroup, and continue later. Fine, but don't give up!

Self-love is another way of celebrating God's creation. When you love and take care of yourself, you honor God. Conceit is different from self-love. Conceit is a lie we tell ourselves and is a separation from God. Conceit is a cover for feelings of worthlessness and fear. Self-love is a right of birth. Unfortunately, self-love can be beaten out of us. All too often it is replaced by fear. Love is with God, and fear is without God. Choosing to love yourself is choosing God.

Self-love can be very tricky. You cannot fully love another person unless you love yourself. People sadly spin their wheels trying to fill the emptiness inside with the love of others. It becomes much like a bottomless glass—the more love they give, the more love you crave. There is no way to satiate the need. The result is twofold: love givers feel resentment because of the constant demand for more love, and recipients of love feel resentment because they are never satisfied.

Why is it that self-love is so difficult? The love we feel from our parents is an external entity that lays the groundwork for us as we grow. Later, we internalize that love and thus create our own self-love. Perhaps as many as 65 percent of births are unplanned, and maybe 45 percent are actually unwanted. Of course, many of those parents do love their babies upon birth, but many do not. For some, the stress of a newborn, another child, is just too great. We love from our overflow; therefore, unwanted children who have not received love from their parents have profound difficulty developing self-love.

Some children garner love through their performance—if they make good grades, if they excel athletically, if they meet parental expectations, then love is the reward. As these children mature, their self-love becomes predicated on conditions and standards they set for themselves. If they succeed, they are able to pat themselves on the back—much as their parents did when they were growing up. However, the standards are often skewed or distorted. Self-condemnation comes easily, but self-love is often not attainable.

Just as we accept the good and bad in our mates and children, so should we be accepting of ourselves. Embracing even the most difficult of emotions, such as shame and anger, is necessary. Your emotions and feelings, no matter how repugnant, are a part of you and do not make you bad or separate you from your decency and higher self.

Remember that your self-concept is the result of your past experiences as well as feedback from important others in your life . . .

For example, you may want to think back to a time when a special friend or teacher told you that you were smart or kind or pretty or handsome, or when an adult or parent complimented you on something you said or did.

Sometimes, however, we give people more power than they deserve and that leads to toxicity. Because someone says something unflattering or critical to you does not mean it is true. So often we tend to incorporate into our belief system the negative things other people say about us. We give them this power because we perceive them to be authority figures or because we love them, so we buy into their views. Anytime people give you toxic feedback, step back and really look at them. Ask yourself why they are motivated to say those things. Just how much of an authority are they? Then make your own assessments. As adults we are more capable of managing that on our own, but when we were children, it was far more challenging. Sometimes we drag those beliefs with us into adulthood, but you can change that. Even just the smallest affirming incidents have a positive impact on our self-image. You may be tempted to dismiss those little moments, but please do not. Thinking back on the positive remarks is important. Such reflections help give us the power to look within and overcome negative and unhappy moments.

The power we give others is an important concept and one we should evaluate often. But our self-image can also be influenced by significant turning points in our lives. Sometimes we are not even aware of these life changes, or we deny them by minimizing their role in our development. Such turning points can be as simple as an off-handed remark or as important as significant milestones such as graduating, taking a new job, marriage, or divorce. Something about these experiences set in motion a very influential mind-set that either spurred you on or tore you down. I would like you to do the following exercise to increase your awareness of how such an experience impacted your self-conception:

1. Think back and describe a turning point experience.
2. Was it positive or negative?
3. How did it impact your self-concept then and now?
4. How much power did you give it?

Many of us have experienced sad and upsetting events in our lives . . .

But you can build on those times, surmounting even the most difficult plight. I am reminded of a patient whom I think of frequently. This young man watched as his mother shot herself to death. At age ten he took total care of his little sister and father, who was a hopeless alcoholic. Finally, relatives (after two years of neglect) put the two children in an orphanage. Their father subsequently died. My patient's sister was adopted but, because he was older and therefore less desirable, he remained in the orphanage until he completed school. While he is a very successful executive today, he wrestles with self-doubt and melancholy. He is married with children and lives next door to his sister, who is also married. Because she was so young at the time of this incident, her adjustment was better. He still vividly recalls the sound of the shot and the memory of his mother's bloody body. He only recently has begun to deal with the anger he feels toward his drunken father, whom he blames for his mother's suicide, and at this juncture, the anger he feels toward his mother is unthinkable.

I have another patient whose mother abandoned him and his brother when he was seven and his brother was three. His father, a cold, remote man, gave no explanation to his children about their mother's disappearance, but within six months of her leaving he remarried an equally cold woman. In the name of discipline, he and his brother were abused and neglected. Eventually, the mother returned and took the younger child, leaving my patient to grieve yet another loss. Today he is married but lives with feelings of inadequacy and anger. Even though he is quite successful, he is troubled by his past. We are working hard together to unravel his anger and to channel it more appropriately. Dealing with anger is imperative to resolving problems. (Session 11 will focus on anger.)

Everyone has challenges, some more painful and difficult than others, but in the process of discovering the genesis of your unhappiness you begin to understand what has happened to you, and this understanding will almost certainly help improve your self-concept. In the process you will gain confidence that can make you soar like an eagle!

The way we were treated as children is often the way we act as adults . . .

Apart from some of the obvious reasons children develop low self-esteem (for example, physical, emotional, and sexual abuse), there are other considerations. Many of you who are working through therapy with me may not have been exposed to really harsh treatment, yet you still battle low self-esteem. Sometimes well-meaning parents unknowingly send destructive messages. One common example is parents who overprotect their children. Overprotection leads a child to develop extreme feelings of anxiety, vulnerability, and learned helplessness. The child interprets Mom's and Dad's vigilance as if life is always full of impending doom, and he or she needs to stay close to the parents for protection. As an adolescent he or she is unable to individuate, see himself or herself as a separate individual, and remains anxious and dependent as an adult. The overprotection makes one feel inadequate and helpless. Domineering parents convey similar attitudes that disallow independent thinking and problem solving.

If you were blessed with parents who showed you unconditional love and approval, chances are you show that to others and feel free to be open about your feelings and thoughts. If you felt accepted as a child, you will act in that fashion as an adult. Most of us develop a picture of ourselves based on how others have treated us, so in a very real sense we are the products of our environment. If you use that as an excuse for your behavior as an adult, however, you are in for a life filled with untruths and pain. There comes a day when we must stand up and be solely accountable for our behavior. This issue is perhaps one of the most difficult with which to grapple in therapy—despite all of the injustices and mistreatments, we now have to let go and say, "That is my past, but I live in and am responsible for the present." The ability to make that statement is also one of the most important growth-producing acts of your free will.

Love is the core of your self-concept . . .

We are all God's creations, so to criticize or loathe ourselves is to criticize or loathe God's work. Once again, we must look at ourselves through God's eyes and shift that self-perception to love and beauty. To see God within us is to accept the cosmos within. Suddenly, where there was weakness, there is strength; where there was ugliness, there is beauty; and where there was darkness, there is light—God's light.

The more you change your idea of yourself, moving to a more positive concept, the more power you create. The more light you allow in, the greater will be your healing. Loving yourself is so essential to your health and growth. According to Marianne Williamson, for example, the way to overcome separation is by healing. Expressions of illness can be seen as separating, isolating, and withdrawing from pain, a denial of self, a moving away from light and love. Paradoxically, this separation, in an attempt to avoid pain, increases it.

Your self-esteem cannot change overnight. Feeling worthwhile comes in pulls and tugs with gradual flashes of insight, but if you work at it, change does come. Our self-image is the summation of learned behaviors, concepts, rules, and experiences, but the self is also dynamic and always changeable. Remember the goal or goals you established in Session 1. With your increased self-awareness and clarification, you have already begun to move to greater heights of personal accomplishment. You can begin to meet your own needs and not live a second-hand life. Start with some self-approval—look at what you are and what you have already achieved and feel proud. You may feel that more work needs to be done, but at least begin with some self-appreciation and love.

List three personal achievements or something about which you are proud. Beside each answer, list the strengths it took to achieve your accomplishments.

	Achievement	Strength
1.		
2.		
3.		

Your self-image—that which defines you—has a profound effect on how people respond to you and you to them . . .

You see the world and others through your own self-filters, and as you gain ground by feeling more valued, the world itself will change to be a sunnier and happier place in which to live. So what do people with high self-esteem look like? They have the following characteristics:

- They have a friendly spirit.
- They are open and communicate their feelings.
- They are flexible and adaptable.
- They are forgiving.
- They are loving and feel lovable.
- They are respectful of themselves and of others.
- They are nice to be around.

These are goals to aim for, and I would bet that if you are kind to yourself and give yourself some room, you are already on your way to achieving these characteristics. But it is of equal importance to be able to help build others' self-esteem—and it is so easy. Something as small as a smile or a kind word to a child or elderly person can be such a boost to them, and it makes you feel good in the process. By practicing these characteristics yourself, you enable the growth of the people around you.

Let's take a look at where you are and how you are communicating to others. Under "Self," rate these characteristics from 1–5, 1 being the least, 5 being the most. Next, give an example about how you have communicated these qualities to others.

Example:

Healthy Self-Esteem	*Self*	*Others*
1. Friendly spirit	3	I am able to show my co-workers I am friendly by speaking kindly.

etc., etc.

Healthy Self-Esteem	*Self*	*Others*
1. Friendly spirit		
2. Communicate feelings		
3. Flexible and adaptable		
4. Forgiving		
5. Loving and feel lovable		
6. Respectful		
7. Nice to be around		

Now list ways that you could improve these seven areas:

Healthy Self-Esteem	Ways to Improve
1. Friendly spirit	1.
2. Communicate feelings	2.
3. Flexible and adaptable	3.
4. Forgiving	4.
5. Loving and feel lovable	5.
6. Respectful	6.
7. Nice to be around	7.

There is a simple exercise I ask of my patients . . .

And, to tell you the truth, I not only have fun teaching it, but I also have fun practicing it. I have a friend who is a former Miss America. We were talking together one day, and in the course of our conversation I asked her if she was able to keep the crown she had been given during the coronation. (Now one of the chief differences between my friend and me is that had I been Miss America everyone would know where that crown is because I would still be wearing it!) Feeling that this opportunity would be as close as I would ever come to the title, I listened intently as Shirley described the crowning. As I was visualizing each detail, suddenly I became Miss America. As a matter of fact, it surprised me how thoroughly involved I became in the fantasy. I felt that if it had that effect on me, it would do something similar for others.

Thus, I began using what I now call "the crown technique" in my practice. When a patient is feeling low and self-deprecating, I ask my patient to close his or her eyes and sit up straight and tall. (Changing your posture is essential—got to keep that crown from falling off!) Then, I ask the patient to reach into a glass container and put the crown on. Now, since I actually do not own a crown, we pretend. Almost immediately the patient begins to feel the specialness of that coronation. This shift in attitude changes the affect or mood. I then suggest to the patient to put the crown on whenever the feelings of self-doubt or discouragement set in. Now, obviously if you go out and actually buy one and start wearing it around, we will need to talk some more, but otherwise this is a great technique that you can pull off any time you need it. If someone criticizes you, "wearing the crown" takes the sting out so that you can evaluate whether what was said is valid (in other words, you can evaluate how much power you are giving this person). If you feel gloomy, put that crown on. If you feel unsure of a situation, crown yourself!

You have the power to make changes and take old beliefs and negative elements of your self-concept and change them. All that is necessary is free choice and openness to our creator. You are in control of your life—no one else is—unless you surrender that control.

Change the I can't to *I can* and the I won't to *I will.*

Session 4 _____

Your Beginnings

_____

Issues we will cover in Session 4:

- **Intrafamilial dynamics** — We'll look at your family patterns and how they have influenced you.
- **Genogram** — This is a family tree that lets you take a unique look at you.
- **Making changes** — You cannot change anyone but yourself.

In our previous session you determined how you see yourself. You considered how a turning-point experience may have affected you. You learned that low self-esteem also can result from childhood experiences other than abuse, such as an overprotective or domineering upbringing. You began the slow process of improving your self-image by listing your achievements and accomplishments. What makes for high self-esteem was reviewed, and you scored yourself in seven areas of healthy esteem. You also listed ways to improve your self-esteem in those seven areas. Finally, you learned how and when to use "the crown technique."

I want to reemphasize how important it is to do these exercises completely and carefully—avoid the temptation to rush your journey. You did not develop overnight the person who you are today, so take the time now to work with me slowly. You will accomplish much more by using a slow and steady approach.

Today I want to talk about your intrafamilial dynamics . . .

If that sounds like an intimidating concept, it really isn't all that complicated. We have already embarked on your intrapersonal dynamics through your needs assessment, beliefs, and personal history. Now we will build on this information in order to fill in those essential blanks that are needed to explain you. We do this by looking at your family (familial) dynamics. In other words, how have things come together to create you and provide definition for you? Looking at your family patterns will help you answer some important questions and will also give you some answers to questions you may have been unable to ask. This particular session may be painful, but I know you can deal with this pain. Psychic pain is a signal that the self is seeking definition.

Families are complicated but are nevertheless necessary to us. Depending on your background, your family has been helpful, supportive, and loving in your development—or tragically unsupportive and damaging. These are only two extremes within a wide range of potential family dynamics. Many people may fall into a neutral or middle ground. For example, in many families there is love and caring but some problems, too. Most families can be graphed like this:

Damaging,   Loving
unloving   _____ supportive,
            1   2   3   4   5   6   7   8   9   10 nurturing

In order to understand you, you must try to understand *your parents*...

As I mentioned before, parents are our first teachers, and their influence on us is pervasive. I believe that the overwhelming majority of parents love their children and really desire to raise them in a healthy fashion. They want their children to feel loved, to feel safe and secure (remember Maslow's needs), and to feel good about themselves.

But these parents all too frequently have needs that were unmet during *their* childhoods, and they have beliefs about themselves that are faulty and painful. They too had parents—parents who were unable to give the kind of unconditional love that they also very desperately needed and who taught your parents how to behave as parents. We spoke before of children who were deprived of love, emotionally scarred, and who now must be able to parent their own children. No one intentionally means to mess up their children, but it happens, and the problems can be traced back through previous generations. We now must become detectives to solve the case of you.

The first exercise that I want you to complete is a genogram . . .

The genogram is another one of those fancy terms that simply means a family tree. Let me show you how to do one. We will use certain symbols to signify relationships and incidents. They are as follows:

The Basic Genogram

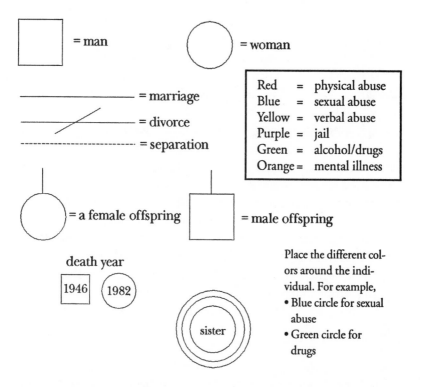

These are the basic tools you use for your genogram. Before you begin drawing though, let's explore an example of what I mean through the case history of one of my former patients.

A forty-two-year-old woman came to see me complaining of depression and loneliness. She was a professional woman and was quite secure financially. She told me that she was divorced and had been single for about eight years. Her former husband was remarried. She was the one who had wanted the divorce and described her former spouse as professionally successful but cold and emotionally distant. He came from a difficult but privileged childhood, as did she. My patient was the mother of two children, both of whom lived with her. At the time of the divorce her son was four years of age and her daughter was six. They are now in their adolescence and giving their mother trouble.

My patient's parents were divorced. Her father just left the family one day with no warning. Her mother had a history of psychiatric problems, and at the age of fourteen my patient was left "to take care of" her mother. Her mother was in and out of mental institutions, suffering from depression, and was often suicidal. My patient had a younger brother, two years her junior, who left home when he was sixteen and is essentially out of her life. Although there were maids to take care of my patient and her brother during their mother's hospitalizations, there were no family members or their father to visit or to help parent them. My patient attended a local college and lived with her mother, and upon graduation, she married. In the beginning this marriage seemed like the answer to all her needs, but not long into the marriage my patient realized that the man whom she had married was as emotionally ungiving as were her parents. The marriage lasted seven years. During those seven turbulent years, my patient's mother continued her frequent hospitalizations and ultimately killed herself in my patient's home. It was soon thereafter that my patient divorced. Like her mother, she now had the task of rearing her children alone.

The children did not handle the divorce very well, and almost immediately the daughter started soiling her pants. At wits' end, the mother dealt with this problem by giving the daughter enemas, which, of course, were quite painful to the child. Amid the tears, screams, and protestations, the girl's young brother watched in horror. After several years, the mother finally received help for her daughter and things began to settle down for a while. As the daughter matured, however, and entered junior high, both she and her brother developed extreme behavior problems. They constantly fought with the mother, both verbally and physically, cut classes, and displayed just general disobedience.

It was at this time that the mother became depressed and sought help from me. By this time the daughter was hearing voices and tried to kill her mother. The girl was hospitalized and diagnosed as having schizophrenia. The brother had a personality disorder, and together with their mother they all remained in therapy. These children had been physically and emotionally abused. Because enemas are often associated with sexual abuse, that too was an issue.

My patient's genogram looks like this:

Patient's Genogram

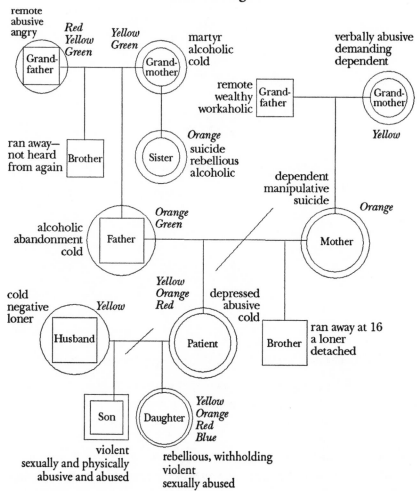

Obviously, few families have this many difficulties, but I use this example to give you an idea of what a genogram looks like. (I did not choose to complete the entire tree for reasons of confidentiality.)

Now I want you to draw your genogram. Include your spouse in the diagram, if you are married or divorced.

Then add your parents and children . . .

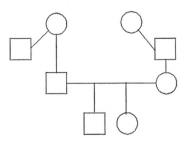

Or, if you are single, begin with your parents and then their offspring, including yourself.

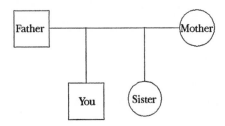

Using the symbols to represent situations and people, draw your tree . . .

After you have completed the drawing, next to each significant person write out three words that best describe your family members. For example, you may want to list both positive and negative descriptors—creative, mean, happy, dependable, afraid, selfish, and so on. (You may notice that I have asked some questions more than once, but always with a different twist. As you grow in the sessions, you will see that your answers change based on what you've learned. So bear with me.)

Next, look at your genogram and ask yourself the following questions. (Write down the answers. *This is important.*)

1. What patterns do I see? (for example: alcoholism, abuse, success, depression, other illnesses)

2. How much divorce exists in my family—none, some, or a great deal?

3. Who am I most like—and who am I least like? Is this someone I admire or dislike?

4. What differences do I see in me and my family members? How am I unique?

5. How is my spouse like a parent or stepparent? Does he or she resemble my father or mother?

6. How is anger dealt with by family members? How do I handle my anger?

7. Who talks to whom in my family?

8. What kind of messages do they send? Are the messages loving?

9. What impact has my family had on my self-concept?

10. What do I see that I need to work on?

Many times when people complete this exercise, they find themselves feeling sad, guilty, or ashamed. The guilt and sadness may be the result of something you feel you did wrong, such as doing drugs or having an abortion. But the shame is generated from something done *to* you—perhaps sexual abuse or verbal abuse or emotional confusion caused by an alcoholic parent. Whether it is something you did or something done to you, dealing with guilt and shame and coming to terms with them will be addressed in Session 9.

No one has a good explanation about why we are born into the families that we are. Why do some people have very blessed childhoods while others suffer terribly? Some people say that it's "the luck of the draw" while others may argue that somehow in a "preexistence" we choose our lot in life in order to learn certain lessons that increase the evolution of our being. Whatever the explanation, we are here now, and this is our reality. We have options, and each decision has the potential for opportunity, growth, and happiness.

I don't believe that our creator makes our pain or is responsible for it. Our creator is there to see us through our darkest hours by providing comfort and solace in our distress and is only a prayer or a thought from our minds and hearts, readily accessible to anyone who asks for spiritual help. Remember that you are part of the creator—the love part.

Making changes and finding support . . .

One way to change a negative influence and keep old tapes from replaying is to break away from people who trigger them. That may seem a bit harsh, but, unfortunately, dysfunctional people commonly gravitate toward one another. Finding new friends is very helpful to enable you to change habits. Get away from those people who reinforce the negatives. But what if this negative trigger comes from a family member? You may want to tell your family that because you are dealing with some important and painful issues, you need some space for a while. With that caveat you can avoid major contact with them until more healing has occurred and you are comfortable with personal boundaries.

Again, we do what we know, but if our behavior is dysfunctional, it merely reinforces old, bad thoughts and feelings. No one is ever going to change unless that person, like you, has made a conscious decision to do so. If you are concentrating on wishing things would be different and for others to change, they won't. You cannot change anyone but yourself—no matter how hard you try. Once you can accept this truth, your growth will take a major surge! So, get away from toxic people.

Next, I recommend that you join a support group such as Emotions Anonymous to help augment the work we are doing. Emotions Anonymous is free of charge and these groups are located in almost every large town or city in the country. Group work really helps, especially when you have done all of this additional groundwork.

If you have never attended a support group, let me tell you more about them. The most highly publicized group is Alcoholics Anonymous, begun many years ago in Akron, Ohio. When I have a patient with substance abuse issues, I will not treat them unless they agree to attend AA. Alcoholics Anonymous offers a twelve-step program toward sobriety that is unmatched. It is by far the best treatment anyone with an alcohol or other drug problem can get. It is confidential—no last names are used—and it is warm and supportive toward any new members.

Offshoots of this beneficial program include Overeaters Anonymous, Alanon for family members of someone with a drug or alcohol problem (alcohol is also a drug), Alateen for teenagers from families with drug abuse, and, of course, the addiction/codependency twelve-step groups. You can locate a meeting place close to you by contacting your local psychiatric hospital. You don't have to give your name; just ask where and when meetings are held. You will feel welcomed by the members but not overwhelmed with attention. The environment is always casual and nonthreatening. Many other groups have been formed to meet specific problems, such as Survivors of Incest, CODA (codependency), Parents Anonymous (parents who have abused their children), Parents without Partners, and a variety of church groups, to name a few.

In this session you have become very aware of your beginnings and how your early life forged your personality. There are theorists today who believe that family-of-origin work is unnecessary. Obviously, I am not one of them. I believe this kind of work is central to the process of change. Your genogram is like a blueprint of your designing influences. It provides you with the knowledge for growth, resolution, acceptance, and forgiveness. Avoid the temptation to blame parents for your problems. They, too, were victims of their own environments. Feeling anger toward them because of their actions is certainly understandable, and it is very obvious that they laid the groundwork for your development. This understanding, however, will aid your growth. It is now time to assume responsibility for allowing yourself to stay stuck and to challenge yourself to move on.

Session 5

Moving from the Pain

Issues we will cover in Session 5:

- **Linear regression** — Access your past.
- **Dysfunctional families** — They're all alike in one way or another and display a pattern of similar beliefs and laws.
- **Hiding secrets** — Troubled families live by certain laws.
- **By-products** — Laws are the behavioral by-product of family laws and include roles of discipline, confusion, and abuse.
- **Enabling personal growth** — You are the only person who can make the decision to live, not just exist.

In Session 4 we learned a great deal about how you grew up and what your family of origin was like by drawing a genogram. You unearthed, perhaps, some painful realities about your parents and were able to trace patterns and character traits from then to now. But I still need to know more about your beginnings, and we will do this through a process called Linear Regression and, then, Family Laws. Closely related to Family Laws is the idea of Family Roles. Roles are the behavioral by-products of Family Laws.

We will now do a technique called linear regression . . .

Put the date of your birth at the top of a piece of paper and list, one after the other, each year following your birth year, up to the present. Look at each date and try to recall an event or memory from that year.

For example,

1954   I was born.

1955

1956   My first sibling was born.

1957   I fell off my tricycle and had to have stitches.

1958   My father got a new job and I got a new puppy.

You probably won't have much recall of the first few years, but you may be aware of things that happened during that time—the birth of a brother or sister, the death of a grandparent, a hospitalization of you or a close relative, unemployment, divorce, separations, and so on. Look back at your genogram to help trigger memories. Also, sometimes reviewing old checkbooks reminds us of particular episodes that may be quite significant. Family picture albums and just picking up the phone to ask "Aunt Tillie" or another family member questions can be very valuable. We are attempting to jar the memory to recall information that will enlighten you about yourself—from the deep recesses of the subconscious to the day-to-day memories at the surface of awareness. Our mind works overtime to protect us from anguish, but unless you are able to access that information, look it squarely in the face, and understand and deal with its collision course on your self-concept, there can be little healing or growth. Being stuck in a no-growth pattern is like a flashlight without batteries. It just doesn't work!

Look at what you've written about your values, rules, and belief system and compare that to the genogram and linear regression. Now write down the patterns, memories, and feelings you are experiencing. Also add your present family (immediate family), so that connecting the past and the present will be easier. If you are single, your friends become your immediate family; so adjust the exercise accordingly.

1. What was it like to grow up in your family of origin?

2. What is it like to be a member of your immediate family?

3. Describe your present relationship with your family of origin.

4. Describe your present relationship with your immediate family.

5. What are the obstacles presented by your family of origin that have interfered with your growth?

6. What are the obstacles presented by your immediate family that interfere with your growth now?

7. Looking at both your family of origin and your immediate family, what issues need to be resolved? What can you do about these?

Troubled families are very much alike . . .

All dysfunctional families, families that have problems and pain, have common characteristics. It is important to understand this principle and to discover that you are not alone and that healing can take place. It's also important to know that even if your family resists any change in you or tells you that you are the one with the problem, that's okay. You are still capable of healing yourself. Dr. Marvel Harrison, Ph.D., and Terry Kellogg are researchers who have outlined Family Rules, which I call Family Laws.[4]

Troubled families live by certain laws . . .

All families have secrets—secrets like gambling, infidelity, substance abuse, physical or sexual abuse, shame over poverty, unemployment, or mental illness. Whatever the problem, families that are dysfunctional want to protect themselves from discovery. The greater the degree of secrecy, the greater the dysfunction and pain. All their energies are directed at hiding and making certain in often quite elaborate ways that the secret remains just that. In their effort to hide their secret, members of the family never or rarely ever speak of the problem. If it is spoken about, it is done in a clandestine whisper, with people pairing off to compare notes. Open exchange of information and sharing of feelings are taboo. One often hears in such families, "We must protect . . . [a certain family member]." The cost of this protection is excessive, often causing everyone involved to be ill, despondent, and angry.

So, the first law in dysfunctional families is: *It is not okay to talk about problems.* Sometimes this law becomes confused with loyalty and presents a distorted view of that concept in adulthood. Obviously, if no one discusses the problem, no help or relief can be obtained. But sometimes, despite the secrecy, one brave family member (usually a child) will start acting out so badly that the family has no choice but to fix things. We call this the "identified patient or problem," and a shrewd healer will recognize the situation immediately. This brave little soul will eventually cause the family to spill the beans!

A second law to which I have already alluded is *Feelings are not expressed openly.* In families with unresolved chemical or codependency issues, this law becomes a nightmare. It is difficult enough to express anger, sadness, despair, but when you are told not to cry (after all, "big boys don't") or touching is not allowed ("don't be such a sissy"), you must stuff your feelings and console yourself in the best way you can. Suppressed feelings have a nasty way of coming to the surface as migraines, ulcers, hypertension, overeating, depression, and anxiety . . . more hiding.

A third law of dysfunctional families is *Communication exists on the surface.* Communication is often indirect, with family members pairing off confidentially or one person, often a child, becoming a messenger for the rest of the family. The obvious danger here is that messages get confused and mixed up. People never say directly to one another what they really mean. The messenger must assume the responsibility for accuracy in the delivery of the message, not to mention the fact that he or she is burdened with the responsibility that "I must fix things." What a position in which to place a child!

This sad situation sets up the next law in dysfunctional families: *Unrealistic expectations—"Make us proud of you!"* In dysfunctional or troubled families, parents often rely on their children to help fill their own needs, so they push and control and demand. "You must always behave, and then I will love you." "You must clean the house so I will be pleased." "You must score the winning point so that I will be proud." Look back at your grandparents to see the origin of these messages that your parents may now be sending you. What I've just described is called vicarious living—the parents live their lives through their child's life. I have tried to teach my children to achieve for themselves and that the grades they earn on school work or any other effort they put forward does not affect my love for them or my self-image.

Unconditional love is essential for helping to build a good self-concept, and if you feel you were not raised with this kind of love, you must understand that you can provide this love for yourself. We all mess up and make mistakes, but making mistakes isn't the end of the world. Mistakes just reveal that we are human! In some families an ideal is created—that old "be-more-like-your-cousin-Nancy" syndrome. Sometimes this ideal resides far from reality, and when you as a child failed to live up to those unachievable standards, you may have felt less than adequate and were ashamed. Love yourself the way you are because that is good enough.

Don't be selfish is another favorite law in painful families. What emerges as a result of this inflexible law is guilt and anger. Anytime a child places her own needs first, the belief within the family is that it is wrong for her to do so. This belief results in individual needs remaining unmet. The stage is set for a dysfunctional, unhappy adult who is never certain about sharing and who goes overboard in one direction or the other, either sharing everything at the expense of her needs and feeling angry, or sharing nothing and feeling defensive and paranoid about being taken advantage of.

There is nothing wrong with taking care of yourself. If you remember from our second session, I told you that we nurture and give to others from our overflow of good feeling. What this means is that if you do not take care of your own needs, you cannot care for others or be a nurturing, loving individual.

And then there is the *Do as I say—not as I do law.* This law teaches three tragic lessons. The first is the double dose of confusion and doubt, and that gives rise to the second, which is an inability to trust. With this law in effect children begin to doubt the truths they are told and to distrust others as well as themselves. With a drink in hand a parent tells a child not to abuse drugs and alcohol, or parents will tell their children an untruth and then admonish them not to lie. What can this child believe!? The third lesson learned from this law becomes a law in itself: *Do what I think others want me to do.* Always trying to please others is like trying to live a double life. If you do not do what you think they want, you fear rejection and ultimately abandonment. If you do behave as you think others wish, you will be constantly uncertain and insecure about your own abilities, feel controlled, and not able to do what you want to do—not a good way to live your life.

Another family law with which we must deal says *It's not okay to play.* People who abide by this law have no child in them or at least no child who can come out to play. They take life seriously at all times, have little humor, and feel that life is about suffering. It is not. Although living can bring pain, life is about joy, happiness, and love. The creator provided us with humor—how else can you explain a gooney bird?! These lovable creatures land and take off in such a way as to make even the most serious person smile with amusement at their shenanigans. If you conduct your-self as solemn and resolute, you may be unable to take risks, and it is risk that can bring you love and fun, folly and pleasure. What happens if you let that inner child out? Do you fear that you may look foolish? I don't think so. Take the risk! It's worth it.

The last law of dysfunctional families is *Don't rock the boat.* Maintain the status quo at all costs—that is what "don't rock the boat" means. This law underlies all of the other seven laws. If you violate the other seven laws, it becomes difficult not to rock the boat. This law is about shame and hiding and about protecting the unhealthy family from being discov-ered. Everyone complies with this law because of fear—fear of loss, anger, shame, and abandonment. It is better to hide the devil we know than to experience the fear of exploring the unknown. In this locked-up existence no growth or healing can take place. There is no room for exceptions, just more pain.

Laws of Dysfunctional Families

Discuss in writing how you were taught by the following laws:

1. **It is not okay to talk about problems.**
   What are they?
   How are the problems covered up?
   What are the secrets?

2. **Feelings are not expressed openly.**
   What feelings were displayed—anger, rage?
   What did you do with pain? and fear?
   What about affection?

3. **Communication exists on the surface.**
   Who spoke to whom?
   What were conversations like?
   How were needs communicated?

4. **Unrealistic expectations.**
   Who expected what from whom?
   What happened to expectations that were unrealized?

5. **Don't be selfish.**
    What belonged to you?
    What were the consequences of taking care of yourself?
    Were your parents selfish?

6. **Do as I say, not as I do!**
    What confusion did this law cost?
    What was the price for you of trying to maintain this law?

7. **It's not okay to play.**
    What was the usual mood around the house?
    What happened if someone was not serious?
    Were you allowed to be a child?

8. **Don't rock the boat.**
    What happened when someone brought up a problem?
    How did your family react to the violation of this law?

Enabling personal growth . . .

Just because your family may be dysfunctional, the family's stagnation and pain need not define you. You can still grow and learn to relate to your family in a healthy fashion by being open, honest, expressing your feelings, and refusing to hide. Change those old laws into healthy ones.

I have said a great deal about laws and about your family, and how you may have become the person you are today should be clear to you by now. All of these things are done without conscious awareness—again, no one intentionally sets out to hurt family members, yet pain and suffering occur over and over. By now you are learning some ways to put an end to the cycle of pain and to begin to live your own life fully. Family and cultural laws teach us how to live and solve problems, and these laws are indeed generational, passing from parent to child on down the line. Look at your patterns of dysfunction and begin by accepting the fearful but growth-producing challenge to change. "We do what we know" is an old adage, but perhaps not a prudent one if we truly are ready to make a difference in our lives. Resolve now to be aware when these laws creep into your consciousness, to take control and create your own healthy laws, such as:

1. It is OK to share a problem openly and honestly with a trusted loved one or spouse.

2. It is important to express feelings truthfully and tactfully.

3. Communication is the way to resolve problems.

4. Expectations should be verbalized and analyzed for fairness and reality.

5. Taking care of yourself allows you to take care of others.

6. Evalutate your behavior for consistency and honesty.

7. Allow yourself the pleasure of play.

8. Love yourself.

Family Roles are the behavioral by-product of Family Laws, as I mentioned previously. . . . Harrison and Kellogg also described the "roles" family members play.[5]

Each of us plays out certain roles in our lives such as Mother, Father, Sister, Friend, Student, Employee, and so forth. Roles are helpful because they acknowledge who we are to ourselves and others. If you are a healthy individual your roles clearly delineate you as a separate individual and allow the expression of your uniqueness. Indeed, you are part of a family and society, but, at the same time, you are different and separate.

If you come from a dysfunctional family, however, your roles are blurred and can be destructive. Roles take on a selective style—not to meet the needs of the individual, but rather to meet the needs of the family. These roles support the prevailing belief system from which the laws were formed. What are truly significant about these roles are the following:

1. They are designed mechanisms to maintain balance in the family.

2. We do not choose the roles we play—these roles are imposed upon us.

3. The price is confusion and loss of identity.

I have categorized some familiar roles people play in dysfunctional families:

Roles of Description	Roles of Confusion	Roles of Abuse
The smart one	The child as caretaker	Sexual abuse victim
The pretty one	The child who parents	Physical abuse victim
The troublemaker	The surrogate spouse	Emotional abuse victim
The good child	The parent who vicariously lives through the child	Toxic religiosity victim
The lazy one	The child as peacemaker	The scapegoat
The over- or under-achiever	The distractor	The rage-er
		The addict

This brief list provides examples of the types of family roles that are used in an effort to hold the family together. Being so caught up—mustering all of your energy to maintain the family—deprives you of achieving self-realization. By thinking about the role you played, and perhaps still do play, you have the opportunity to see your pain and stop the pattern. Even in the most troubled families, there seems to be a strong desire to preserve the unit. Family members are striving to meet those early needs of survival and belonging, even at the extreme cost of abuse and illness.

What roles do you play? . . .

Think back over your childhood, and for each category identify at least one role you played as well as roles played by each member of your family.

Roles of Description	Roles of Confusion	Roles of Abuse

Now ask yourself the following questions (and write out the answers):

1. Who gave you that role?
2. How did you feel about it—then and now?
3. What roles do you and your family-of-origin members play now?
4. What has been the price?

It is helpful at this point to look at characteristics of healthy families. . . . Again we look to Harrison and Kellogg.[6]

As you look at the following list, score your family and see where work is needed:

	My Family				
	Most of the time		Sometimes		Never
1. A healthy family is highly expressive of feelings (both positive and negative), generally reflects a warm and caring tone, demonstrates respect and understanding of each other, and deals with conflict early and effectively.	5	4	3	2	1
2. Parents are in charge and this law is understood by the children.	5	4	3	2	1
3. Spouses feel free to reveal to each other hidden thoughts, intense feelings, or daring ideas without fear of censure or anger.	5	4	3	2	1
4. Important family values are modeled and demonstrated by the parents in their actions and responses.	5	4	3	2	1
5. Parents behave as responsible leaders; children are not expected to be miniature adults.	5	4	3	2	1
6. Family members are receptive to and discuss others' feelings and thoughts.	5	4	3	2	1

7. Family members respect each   5   4   3   2   1
   other's unique characteristics and
   ideas; it's okay to be different.

8. The family approaches problem   5   4   3   2   1
   solving with an emphasis on
   negotiation, give and take, search
   for consensus, willingness to
   compromise.

Unfortunately people don't change until the pain is so great that they can no longer stand it. You may have reached that point. Remember, the only person that you can change is *you*. The other people in your life will have to make their own decisions about changing. This may mean that you must go your own way without them because trying to fix someone else is just not possible and only creates more dysfunction. It's time to take care of you. Remember, trust and climb!

The following words were inscribed on a wall of an underground tunnel found in Cologne, Germany, after World War II. The author is unknown.

I Believe in the Sun

I believe in the sun, even when it isn't shining;
I believe in love, even when there's no one there.
And I believe in God even when He is silent.

I believe in miracles.
I believe in light.
I believe there can always be a way.
I believe that nothing is impossible,
That all things are possible with God.

Healing

Session 6 _____

Mind–Body

_____

Issues we will cover in Session 6:

- **Nexus of mind and body** — This connection can't be broken, and becoming aware of this fact is your path to well being.
- **Necessity for love, maintaining hope, and finding meaning in life** — We literally can't live without these important expressions of our human nature.
- **Will, the action part of hope** — *Will* is the verb that empowers hope.
- **Abuse and illness** — You may be suffering from a legacy of dysfunction and pain, which is the underpinning of many psychological and physical disorders.
- **The Environment** — I will help you make your physical environment a haven and fill your emotional environment with good relationships.
- **Implications of stress** — Stress has a definite impact on illness.

In Session 5 you created a linear regression to enable you to gain insight into your past. Then we discussed dysfunctional families and the common laws they all seem to follow. You wrote about your experiences with the laws established in your family and gained further insight by identifying the roles you may have played to support those family laws and belief systems. Finally, you scored your family on a test that helped you understand characteristics common to healthy families. By now you should have a pretty clear indication of where your family-of-origin work should occur.

Let's begin this session by discussing the mind–body connection . . .

Those of us who have been in medical or mental health practice for even a few years are quick to recognize the connection between the mind and the body. This link is vital because how the two interrelate can make us sick or well, successful or failures. Modern medicine with all of its heralded and well-deserved praise cannot "make" a person well who does not wish to be well. We have at our disposal a whole array of techniques, medications, and procedures to diagnose carefully and treat even the most profound physical or mental illness, but with all of these assets we can do little if the patient believes in or desires a negative outcome. That may sound a bit heavy, but a look at the history of healing, before penicillin, steroids, and anesthetics, will reveal that good doctors knew their patients and treated them holistically. These early doctors did some old fashioned talking, empathized with their patients, and gave generously of themselves. Before the word *stress* was even a medical concept, these healers wanted to know about the patient's home life, about issues of their family of origin, about the patient's job or career, finances, family illness, hopes, disappointments, and dreams.

There are doctors in both the fields of medicine and psychology who hold that people create their own illness, unhappiness, and failure, that we somehow allow ourselves to become sick. Perhaps by thinking certain thoughts and holding certain beliefs you do somehow invoke sickness into your life, physically or emotionally, not to mention failure and pain. The world is like a mirror, and our seeing pain, dishonor, hatred, and prejudice often may be simply a reflection of what is going on inside of us. These afflictions are the opposite of God, and the cures come as we change our minds and hearts. I mentioned previously that some people believe that perhaps a bargain is struck with God in a preexistence to be carried out in life so that a disorder or problem can teach something and is dealt with in order to learn and experience more light. I do believe that the genesis of disease, whether in the body or in the mind, is a combination of factors that includes the following:

- lack of love
- absence of hope
- lack of meaning
- abuse
- feelings

- environment
- heredity
- loss of self-esteem
- stress

The impact that lack of love has on the individual has been well documented . . .

Anyone who has taken the most elementary course in psychology has read about the infant mortality during World War II. Infants were taken out of cities that were being heavily bombed by the Germans and moved into the mountains for safety. Startling accounts of deaths among these babies were reported even though these infants were safe, healthy, fed, and sheltered. The responsibilities of their British nurses were stretched beyond reason and allowed them only enough time to attend to the basic needs of these youngsters. Without touch and affection babies turned their faces to the wall and died.

Experiments have been conducted with Rhesus monkeys that also support evidence of this basic need for love. In some of these experiments the monkeys were reared in isolation from their true mothers but were permitted to feed from and cling to artificial mothers. Two different types of "laboratory mothers" were provided with devices that permitted the young monkeys to obtain milk by sucking. Both "mothers" were immobile and, although they had torsos, heads, and faces, they bore little resemblance to real monkey mothers. One of the laboratory models was constructed of wire so that, while the young monkey could cling to it, this "mother" could scarcely be described as "cuddly." The other, covered with terry cloth (Turkish towel variety) over the wire frame, was more "cuddly" than the wire model.

The experiment was designed to determine if one mother was always the source of food, would that feeding mother be the one to which the young monkey would cling? The results were dramatic: No matter which mother was the source of food, the infant monkey spent his time clinging to the terry cloth "cuddly" mother. This purely passive but soft-contact mother served as a source of psychic security for the monkey. These experiments underscore the extreme need that all babies have to be nurtured and loved. Children who are deprived of love and nurturing then grow up with personality disorders and are unable to feel and give love themselves. They wander through many relationships, never feeling any fulfillment, always needing more, seeking and yearning, feeling angry and deprived. Their inner child still craves that early love and tenderness.

I believe it is difficult to separate lack of love and absence of hope . . .

The two seem to be intrinsically linked. A classic example of the phenomenon of absence of hope is graphically yet beautifully described by one of my personal heroes, Dr. Viktor Frankl, in his remarkable book *Man's Search for Meaning.*[7] Dr. Frankl tells us of the human atrocities that the Nazis imposed on German Jews in the concentration camps of Germany. Frankl chronicles a detailed account of life in those bastions of horror that relates the suffering, the physical and mental pain and anguish, the filth, starvation, and brutality, and, ultimately for some six million people, death.

Frankl asks the question, how does one survive these horrors? His answer is woven into the fabric of what he calls "logo therapy." Succinctly put, Dr. Frankl believes that if some hope and meaning can be realized from all of the pain, humans can rise above their immediate, tumultuous reality and become suspended in faith. He saw prisoners come into the camps, some in good condition, but because they were unable to maintain the hope and meaning of life, they gave up quickly and died. He saw others whose determination superseded all other thoughts, and they managed to survive. The difference between some of these people can perhaps be explained by their mental outlook and strength, their faith and purpose in life. Love, hope, and will made them survivors and were the substitutes for good nutrition, medicine, and humane treatment.

I think that hope may be another way to express meaning . . .

We talked a bit in the preceding sessions about finding meaning in life, but I feel a need to strengthen that idea within you. In the absence of hope and love, babies and adults die, as we have discussed. In the absence of meaning we become selfish, narcissistic beings with insatiable needs and wants, and this is actually just another form of death. On a holy day two thousand years ago a man named Jesus made a difference by dying on the cross. Long before his suffering and death, his life embodied meaning. It was about setting an example for all of us to follow, about being selfless and giving to others. Whether one agrees that he is the savior is immaterial. Differing beliefs do not detract from his great humanitarian work. His lessons about life, however expressed, should not go unheeded.

Jesus' meaning in life was to save humanity so that upon death we will realize the light and love of God. Our life's meaning may not be this dramatic, but we each have the opportunity to discover what that meaning can be. Sometimes I think it is very difficult indeed to focus on what our lives mean, to find what purpose we each serve, but it is essential to our mental health to pursue this important issue. Please let me give you some examples about meaning.

I do not believe that we are expected to be like, for example, Albert Schweitzer. I believe that our meaning is usually far less complex. All of my life I have had two critical interests—one was to have a family, and the second was to pursue my interest in mental health. Obviously, that is why I am writing this book and why I became a doctor. Likewise, my children are the most important people in my life, and I feel that part of my life's meaning is to raise them to be good, kind, and decent people and to help them to achieve that end.

So my point is that part of my mission, my life's meaning, is to rear my three wonderful children and to help others through my professional skills. I also know that along the way other events will occur to change, alter, and add to my meaning, but I have faith that I will continue to try to meet the challenges.

My message is simple—you do not have to invent the formula for world peace to have meaning in your life. Your meaning is right in front of you. It may be that your meaning, like mine, is to rear your children or be active in your community or help a friend or elderly person. Life's meaning is not something nebulous or exotic. It is about being kind and respectful to others and to yourself. It is taking care of yourself and unraveling the problems that confront you. It is becoming more genuine and giving and learning to love yourself. Until there is self-love, there is not room for anything else. Perhaps you have been struggling for years to make sense out of your life and to rise above guilt and shame. When you find meaning, the struggle is lessened.

How to find your meaning and purpose . . .

God did not create a meaningless world. Accepting that concept and building on it implies that God also did not create meaningless life. It is easy for us to acknowledge that the purpose of the simplest forms of life (amoebas and protozoans) is for them to be part of the food chain, to sustain more complex forms of life, and that everything else God created exists as he created it. And that includes us. My previous analogy does not demand a leap in faith, nor should the ideas of meaning and purpose in each of our lives. Clearly, we are all part of an enormous spiritual plan, and we each have a specific and unique meaning to discover for ourselves. We make the world we live in, and we shape our future to a large extent by the choices we make.

I have made some very painful mistakes in my life, but I am able to deal with them because I know that God has forgiven me, and, of equal importance, what I learned from the sadnesses has prepared me for my next level of awareness. Each step of my life and of yours is prepared by the steps that come before. Each person who enters our lives teaches us a lesson. From the moment of our conception to the present time we build upon each experience, good or bad. In Session 5 I asked you to develop a time line of events that punctuated your life. To help you find meaning, go back to your past and ask yourself these questions:

Why Am I Here?

1. What teachers did I meet at each juncture?
2. How did they help or hinder me?
3. What did loss teach me?
4. What did success teach me?
5. What themes or patterns are there?
6. How did one event lead to another?
7. Who introduced me to whom?
8. What has been the outcome of some of these sometimes trivial meetings and events?
9. How do I describe my pain and joy, my thoughts and actions.
10. When did I feel God?

Our lives are about trying to love unconditionally and serving others. Your meaning may be a bit hazy to you, or your meaning may not be clear at all until the end of our time together, but I believe this: as you walk your journey through the remaining sessions, your meaning will be revealed. There is an ancient Oriental expression that says, "When the pupil is ready, the teacher will come." Each experience—the trials and tribulations—was predicated on another experience; one event follows the next event until you arrive at this point. As you go through your time line, you will discover common threads—teachers, family members, and friends—

that played a crucial role in your development. How much happier your life would be if you decided to share the message of hope rather than despair, to give of yourself even in the smallest way to help another, to render encouragement and friendship. Love takes less energy than hate and flows more naturally. When we are conscious of our existence, the call to discover meaning and purpose follows. Once you have begun the process to identify those purposes, honor them and spiritually watch as light directs your life.

Will is actually hope in action . . .

Some people, because of a lack of meaning or an absence of hope, give up all too quickly when they are confronted with failure, disease, or emotional problems. If you tend to fall into this category, let me share with you a phenomenon called spontaneous remission, or self-healing. Only in the last fifteen years or so have scientists begun to probe this mystery, although it has been documented since the beginning of recorded medicine. Sometimes a patient will receive the terrifying news that despite all available efforts there is no chance of a cure for the illness and that it is time to put affairs in order. This news always comes on the heels of solid evidence that reveals the advance of their disease. Lengthy laboratory studies have been done and, in many cases, even surgery, so there is absolutely no doubt that the diagnosis is accurate. The patient is informed of the prognosis and is given six months to live, and the physician doesn't expect to see this terminally ill patient again.

Time goes on and the patient shows no signs of deterioration. On the contrary, he or she seems to be fit as a fiddle, happily doing what he or she wishes without complaint. Then, upon a repeat examination, the cancer or disease is miraculously gone. There is no explanation. The patient simply is no longer sick. While this situation does not happen routinely, it occurs often enough so that scientists are looking into the phenomenon. What in the world so profoundly changed this patient from doom to bloom? I believe it has to do with will and hope. Sometimes these people report making a complete change of lifestyle, from stoically suffering daily corporate stress to pursuing daily relaxation on a sandy beach. Others may report a change in their family or personal relationships. Whatever the result, the common denominators that instigated change are hope and will.

Using psychological testing, we can predict with a high degree of accuracy who will get cancer, what type, and even the outcome. That is a pretty strong, even unbelievable, assertion—but true. Most people have read about the connection between the survivors of cancer and their personality styles. One of the most important characteristics among the survivors seems to be the individual desire to live—to fight back and to refuse to accept the inevitable. Closely linked to that desire is the ability to feel joy. Sometimes even those who fight back hard eventually must give up their battle, but statistics consistently show that this group outlives other patients with the same type and degree of cancer but who lacked the fighting spirit.

Will is the verb that empowers hope . . .

And *will* can be the verb that empowers you, regardless of your circumstances. Just consider that it took Thomas Edison ten thousand experiments to discover the light bulb, and it took Abraham Lincoln four defeats, one bankruptcy, and two nervous breakdowns to become president of the United States. *Will,* the action part of hope, is what did it. Failing does not mean capitulation; it simply means not achieving your goal *just yet.* There are no time limits on attempts, unless you put them there. "Try, try again" is an old American adage that has served us well throughout our history and can serve you well throughout yours. One of my favorite poems captures the essence of will—

Invictus

Out of the night that covers me,
Black as the Pit from pole to pole,
I thank whatever gods may be
For my unconquerable soul.

In the fell clutch of circumstance
I have not winced nor cried aloud.
Under the bludgeonings of chance
My head is bloody, but unbowed.

Beyond this place of wrath and tears
Looms but the Horror of the shade,
And yet the menace of the years
Finds, and shall find, me unafraid.

It matters not how strait the gate,
How charged with punishments the scroll,
I am the master of my fate;
I am the captain of my soul.[8]
—William Ernest Henley

If you believe in yourself and put will into action, your powers are infinite!

Abuse is next on our list of disease-causing factors . . .

The connection of abuse with disease has been well documented. A disturbing reflection of this fact is recognition of the number of patients suffering from multiple-personality disorders as the result of sexual abuse in childhood. Abuse does not need to be sexual, however, to cause damage. Verbal abuse, physical abuse, sexual abuse, and neglect are all lethal. Children who are told how disappointed their parents are with them, that they are dumb, stupid, and useless, give up and quite often fulfill their parents' damaging predictions. These children grow into angry adults, often depressed, not understanding why life just does not seem to bring any pleasure or peace of mind. They often drop in and out of marriages, careers, and friendships, never able to keep things together, and longing for the intimacy that eludes them. Such is the legacy of verbal abuse.

Abuse can often be so terrifying and traumatic that some people find escape by developing other personas within the self—personalities that are better able to cope with the horror. Only through intensive psychotherapy can these personas be integrated into one whole person. As with sexual and verbal abuse, physical abuse destroys the child's sense of trust and incapacitates the sense of self, leaving deep and pervasive scars in the psyche. I treated a youngster who was hospitalized for over a year and of whom I became very fond. Billy was a street kid, into drugs, truancy, physical altercations with peers. Eventually he was admitted to a psychiatric hospital for substance abuse. When he was a baby, his biological father would throw him up against the wall and beat him. I believe that this abuse, coupled with the drug use, caused brain damage, just to add another burden to his list of problems.

Billy was a sweet kid and loved his mother; however, she too had come from a history of abuse. At age seventeen she became pregnant with Billy. She divorced Billy's father—who was ultimately sent to jail for armed robbery—and then she went from man to man. Billy's home life was extremely dysfunctional: his narcissistic mother regarded him with contempt and felt burdened by the responsibility of parenting. At fourteen Billy often lived on the streets with little or no food and would make desperate attempts to move back with his mother. She felt he was incorrigible and a liability to her lifestyle. She would go months without visiting him in the hospital, always promising in phone calls to come but never showing up. Billy found it unacceptable to admit his anger toward her as he clung to some misguided hope that she would rescue him. Confrontation with her was too much of a risk. Finally, when he was discharged, she agreed to let him move back in, but it was only for a short time. She soon threw him out on the streets again, back to drugs. He committed suicide. Billy had no will to live and, without his mother's love, no desire or hope.

Abuse is perhaps the most critical issue with which I must deal in my practice, and it happens to people regardless of race, religion, education, and social strata. Abuse is the underpinning of many psychological disorders, and if you have been a victim of this terror, please understand that the people who did this to you were wrong in their behavior and very ill. You are a good person. This is a very difficult concept to get across because abused children grow up feeling that in some way they caused the problem and that they deserved the treatment they received. Nothing could be further from the truth. Their self-concept becomes inundated with self recriminations such as "I am not smart"; "I am not worthy"; "I am nobody"; I don't deserve . . ."; "I am bad"; "I am not lovable."

I am here to tell you that these are only words, not truths, and that you can turn things around through self-love. Appreciate yourself and your strengths. This goes for abused people and for those who are not abused. List five positive statements about yourself right now, and under each write an affirmation. An affirmation is a way to feed the subconscious positively. You may use this model:

STATEMENT: I am honest.
AFFIRMATION: I respect and cherish my abilities to be an honest reliable person.

1. STATEMENT: _____

   AFFIRMATION: _____

2. STATEMENT: _____

   AFFIRMATION: _____

3. STATEMENT: _____

   AFFIRMATION: _____

4. STATEMENT: _____

   AFFIRMATION: _____

5. STATEMENT: _____

   AFFIRMATION: _____

One of the ways to avoid or overcome disease is by healing old wounds. If you have been abused, it is so very important to talk about this issue with a professional counselor. While our book sessions can help, they do not take the place of a one-to-one, in-person psychiatric session. There are also support groups that help these issues of abuse, and Session 10 on "therapy from the soul" will be of great help. Though the road is bumpy, you *can* overcome your past.

Now, let's discuss the function of feelings . . .

I mentioned earlier that I believe that we are each our own co-creator. Part of the mechanism by which this miracle occurs is through chemicals in the body that allow the mind and body to communicate. Some of these chemicals may be ones you have heard about, such as endorphins, interleukins, and, of great importance, peptides. These chemicals are triggered by your feelings, so obviously the more positive feelings one communicates to the body and mind, the more positive chemicals will be secreted. In other words, you control how you will react, behave, and perhaps heal. Again, I must stress that other variables such as heredity do have an impact, but what is terribly important to understand is that research suggests that you really are your own co-creator, thanks to feelings. And those feelings become chemicals!

Identifying feelings can be challenging for several reasons. Because some people grow up never thinking in terms of feelings, they have difficulty matching thoughts with emotions. Feelings are a response to an event or an experience, but sometimes we confuse someone else's feelings with our own. For example, a child may take on feelings of anger or fear that really belong to her parent, or an adult may adopt the spouse's feelings. Understanding what is truly your feeling and allowing yourself fully to own and experience it can lead to problem solving. Suppressing feelings can lead to disease, yet out of fear of their actions, some people do just that. Just because you have a feeling such as anger does not mean you must act it out.

How many feelings can you identify? Most people can come up with only a few, such as good, bad, happy, unhappy. It is vital to your health, however, to understand, identify, and recognize feelings. Take a few minutes to consider as many feelings as you can think of. Here is a list of possibilities:

Feelings List

sad	despair	panic
apologetic	surrender	content
anger	worry	jealousy
rage	embarrassment	hurt
anxiety	paranoid	insecurity
fear	arrogant	lonely
guilt	bashful	light hearted
shame	bored	ecstatic
humiliation	envious	hopeful
frustration	happy	skeptical
joy	optimism	enthusiasm

Now it's your turn to make your own list about how you've been feeling lately:

_____

_____

_____

Feelings are a vital link between health and dysfunction. Negative feelings, such as hopelessness and helplessness, activate neurally regulated, biological emergency patterns that lower the immune system. Conversely, positive feelings, such as joy and optimism, activate neurally regulated, biological health patterns that empower the immune system! If you needed to refer almost completely to the list of feelings rather than just listing how you feel off the top of your head, it's time to do some work. If you are uncertain about your feelings, your actions will reflect that uncertainty. Here's some help. Try writing a few sentences telling about the time you felt the following:

loved: _____

_____

_____

_____

lonely:_____

_____

_____

_____

rejected:_____

_____

_____

_____

afraid:_____

_____

_____

_____

Feelings, good or bad, need to be expressed. If they are not expressed, they get stuffed down inside of us and cause us to experience failure, disease, and pain. But why are we so afraid of feelings? It can go all the way back to childhood and what you were taught about open expression. Writing can help you to be more aware of what you are feeling:

What are you feeling now?_____

_____

_____

How does being aware of your feelings help you? _____

_____

_____

What did your parents teach you about feelings in general? _____

_____

_____

What did your parents teach you about expressing your feelings?

_____

_____

Anyone who has ever been around a two-year-old can vouch for that child's ability to express feelings. In the previous exercise you told me how feelings were dealt with when you were growing up. What happened between the time you were two and the age you are now? Your parents, perhaps without you even being aware of it, gave you messages about which emotions are okay to express and which are not. If your parents told you anger was bad, you learned to suppress it. If sex was a taboo, you probably still have discomfort talking about that subject. If your parents only expressed superficial emotions, nothing deep or personal, you may be relating at a similar emotional depth. If you have trouble identifying your feelings, I want to share a helpful technique. Whether your goal at the beginning of this book was to achieve healing, success, or peace, this exercise will help put you in better touch with yourself. Your body sends you messages, and it is time to listen.

1. First, get comfortable in a quiet place and close your eyes. Take two deep breaths.

2. We will be taking an imaginary trip through your body, and I want you to visualize first your feet. How do they feel? Are they comfortable, do they hurt? Feel the sensation.

3. Next, slowly move up to your legs and become very aware of how they feel. Are your muscles relaxed? Do your legs feel heavy?

4. Now, move up your body and be aware of your back, stomach, shoulders, arms, neck, and face.

5. Now, let's go inside your head and see how it feels there in your mind. Does it feel dark, light, heavy? What is going on inside?

6. Now that you have gone from your feet to your head, be aware of any part of your body that is sending you messages. Is there pain or tension anywhere? What is your body telling you?

7. Now, it is time to ask your body how you feel? Ask yourself, what is it like inside of me?

8. Finally, think for just a minute of an uncomfortable situation, something that has upset you. Hold on to it for thirty to forty seconds.

Now where are you feeling it? Does it make your head hurt, give you back pain, upset your stomach?

That is your body communicating with your mind and with you! Becoming aware of this communication will help you find the healing you deserve. Accept your feelings — accept yourself.

One's environment, both the physical and emotional aspects, are further factors that I believe can cause disease . . .

The most obvious environmental factor is one's physical working and living conditions. Do you live in or work in an area that has low levels of pollution, noise, and stress? Do you live in an area that prizes clean air, exercise opportunities, and good food? We are all familiar with the incidence of lung disease among some miners or the consequences of high stress imposed by some types of employment. Physical environmental issues can be dealt with—you can move or change jobs—but what about your emotional environment? There is little one can do about one's past. The past is—well, past! It cannot be changed. If you came from a family that was abusive, neglectful, unloving, and limiting, it is now behind you, and although I would like you to do some grieving over this loss, I also want you to move on. We live in the present. Please answer the following questions. (You may be surprised to see what you tell me!)

1. What is your emotional environment now?

2. Have you done your best to make your home loving and accepting? If you haven't, it is time to do so. List some ways to achieve this (for example, cleaning, changing furniture around, inviting friends over, and so on).

    a.

    b.

    c.

3. What about your love life? Ask yourself, is my mate warm, reassuring, loving, and nurturing?

4. Why do I remain in this relationship? Is it helpful or hurtful?

5. Are my needs being met in this relationship?

6. Am I growing—or suffocating?

Another aspect of your emotional environment is friends and relationships outside your family. Having someone in whom you can confide is essential to good mental health. I think that most people require one or two close, intimate friends, and then one needs friends who are more casual and with whom one may share some common interests but not emotional intimacy. Many people, because of their sense of inadequacy and low self-esteem, find it difficult to make friends. One way to combat that problem is to admit to potential friends that perhaps you are a little shy. Upon hearing this, most people will go out of their way to make you feel welcome. This, in turn, bolsters your self-worth and makes you more open to others. Sometimes patients tell me that they don't know where to find friends. I have several safe suggestions beginning with support groups, churches, and civic clubs. There are always nice people to be found among these groups.

Your home environment needs to be a haven. A place where you go to relax, unwind, and feel safe. It should be open only to people who care about you and who are supportive. (So maybe it would be wise to meet your mother-in-law some place else for lunch! You need to take care of yourself!)

The heredity factor . . .

The genes we inherit from our parents, grandparents, and so on down the line play a key role in our health. Science has become increasingly aware of the importance of genetic predisposition in diseases, which include cancer, heart disease, diabetes, depression, schizophrenia, and hypertension, to name just a few. An integral part of treatment is a thorough medical history. But identifying your genetic makeup is not the complete picture.

What is interesting about genetics is that not all genes are expressed and not every member of the family inherits the bad ones. There are some people whose genetic background seems to suggest impending doom for them, yet they remain healthy and fit. No scientific explanation is known for this phenomenon. There are characteristics, however, that healthy people have in common. Healthy people —

- seem to manage stress very well
- are active and have family ties and friends
- find life adventuresome and tend to view problems as challenges
- practice good health habits and take care of themselves
- have a high degree of self-love and believe in a higher power.

A giant threat to good health is low self-esteem . . .

Low self-esteem is what we have been talking about all along. I believe that sometimes people open themselves to failure and emotional disorders through their negative attitudes and poor self-image. People who do not value themselves tend to reflect this in their appearance, attitude, and speech. Some people almost invite disease through their habits, such as smoking, drugs and alcohol, poor diet, and obesity, just to name a few. Their speech is filled with body talk. "So and so is a pain in the neck." "He broke my heart." "I feel I have lost my mind." "I am spineless." They court disaster and then are appalled at the suggestion that maybe they played a major contributing role in their own disease!

I do not believe that destiny means something beyond our control. We create our own destiny, either good or bad. Relying on the excuse of destiny is the antithesis of exercising free will. I believe that we are capable, because of low self-value, to lay the groundwork for maladies. I have a friend who never has a cold. At the first onset of a symptom he sits down and tells his body all the reasons why a cold is irrational and, in so doing, communicates with his subconscious, which actually may be giving him messages to slow down a little. There is an expression that goes, "We get what we deserve." I disagree with that saying, but I do believe that often "We get what we want." The next time that you don't feel well, you may want to try what my friend with the good self-image recommends. Talk to yourself and ask: What benefits can I achieve from a cold? It may be that you just need some nurturing or a little time off. Another way to visualize the concept of exercising your free will is—God gave you the airplane with which you must navigate, no matter how bumpy the ride.

I am honored to count Kent Waldrep[9] as one of my friends. About eighteen years ago, during a Texas Christian University football game,

Kent incurred a spinal injury that left him paralyzed from the neck down. His reaction to this tragedy has been to fight back, and his determination to lead a normal life and to help others is inspirational. Four years after the injury, Kent fought all obstacles to go to Russia for some controversial treatment. His doctors warned Kent and his parents that claims about this treatment just gave false hope. Kent went anyway and did regain some feeling and motion in his arms and hand. Kent is happily married today and has two wonderful little boys. Kent's will is so strong and his meaning is very clear. Through his two foundations and the research they fund, he has paved the way for other spinal cord patients. Kent drives his own van and travels all over the world raising funds and educating others.

Kent was raised by two loving parents, who always believed in him—so Kent learned to believe in himself. It is a combination of his positive self-esteem and sheer gutsy grit that has made him a giant among men.

The last factor that I want you to look at is stress . . .

Stress has become the heralded disease of our modern era even though it is an integral part of what it means to be human. Stress has been with us since the dawn of humanity. Just think of the stress that must have plagued the prehistoric hunter facing down a saber-toothed tiger with only a club and his wits!

The insights I have gained through research and treating patients lead me to believe that focus on stress—controlling it, learning to manage it, and making it work for you—will be the cutting edge of medicine in the 90s. Stress is the trigger on the gun that riddles your life with disease, emotionally and physically. In our next session we will devote the entire time to stress. When I opened our discussion in this session, I listed what I believe are the contributing factors to, or even the genesis of, illness. They are

- lack of love
- absence of hope
- lack of meaning
- abuse
- feelings
- environment
- heredity
- loss of self-esteem
- stress

Perhaps another way to express this might be the following: Because stress acts as a catalyst, I believe it is a precursor to the following contributing factors to disease:

Stress

- lack of love
- absence of hope
- lack of meaning
- abuse
- feelings

- environment
- heredity (expressed genetically)
- loss of self-esteem
- stress

We will talk more about stress and de-stressors in the next session. This session has been all about the mind-and-body connection, what makes us ill, and what makes us well. With love, hope, and meaning we express our humanness, and then we are able to turn from darkness to light!

The Self Under Stress

Issues we will cover in Session 7:

- **Stress** — Stress is not just disease inducing, it's also vital for healthy motivation.
- **Effects of personality on stress** — We all deal with stress differently, but by identifying the personality styles of yourself and others, you can minimize the impact of stress.
- **De-stressors** — I'll give you some tools you can begin using immediately.
- **Interpretation Loop** — By understanding this loop and combining it with the Accuracy Mechanism and Choice Mechanism, communication as well as decision making become easy: P-E-I = $(P_R\ B_R)$ + (AM + CM) = P!

In Session 6 we explored the connection between the mind and the body. You learned how vital love, hope, and meaning are to your life and that you can use your free will to overcome disease, either physical or emotional. Then, I introduced the concept of stress, which we will now address.

You would probably agree that the relationship between stress and disease is not just casual . . .

You would possibly also agree that stress in and of itself does not always lead to illness. Good stress, I believe, may be part and parcel of—or even actually synonymous with—motivation. So, if we look at the doers in our society, we may be looking at people who make stress work to their advantage.

The more complex your lifestyle, the more juggling you are asked to do. I see a lot of women in my practice who are at their breaking point because they place upon themselves Herculean demands that would make three people hard pressed to accomplish. The typical history goes like this: They are married and have several children. They have the responsibility of taking care of home and children; in addition, they compete in stress-provoking jobs or careers. Their day begins around 5:30 A.M. as they prepare themselves for work and get the children off to daycare or school. Next, they rush off to their jobs, often making a long, traffic-snarled commute. They are deluged with work at their jobs, often too overloaded to take a break, and many times skip lunch to run family errands. In the back of their minds are the children's needs: dealing with baby-sitters, car pools, soccer games, Boy Scouts and Girl Scouts, and the evening dinner. When they finally come home, the evening is filled with catching up on household chores, helping with homework, baths, family schedules, and trying to find a little time for "family life." Of course, in between, cars need repair, kids get sick—not to mention the dog— and when I ask these women what they do for themselves, they look at me as if I have lost my mind!

Doing something for themselves is a very alien concept to these women. One of the first things I do is ask such a patient to stand up and turn her back to me. I then make the comment that I can't find the red "S" on her back. They then sit down and begin telling me about marital problems, or a husband who has left the family, or alcoholism, unemployment, abuse, and problems with a child. The companion emotions are fear, guilt, and feeling overwhelmed. "Supermom" is in trouble.

The men who come to see me often have a parallel history, but with some variations. They tend to focus more on their career demands, business issues, employer–employee conflicts, frustrations and concerns for the future. Sometimes they are the single breadwinners, or they have been left by their wives and are trying to raise children on their own. In our society we rear women to be caregivers and men to fix things. When a man is confronted with situations he can't fix—the economy, a sick child, a wife's needs—he often becomes angry, frustrated, and then withdraws into himself.

The difference between those people who control stress and those people whom stress controls is often defined by our perceptions. Dr. Keith Schnert[10] offers one definition of stress and says it is "an imbalance between perceived demand of a stressful event and the perceived response capabilities of the individual, which results in difficulties in coping, and begins the degenerative compromise of the immune system, resulting in illness." Let me illustrate this:

Same Event — Different Perceptions

Person A	Person B
I feel totally overwhelmed. I am unsure of my ability to deal with this crisis. It is just too much—so what's the use. Boy, does my head hurt. I feel like I am going to explode!	This situation is a big challenge— but I have dealt with worse, so I am up for it. I've always managed in the past, so I can conquer this one as well. I feel energized and enthusiastic!

Despite our fantasies, no one can live without stress. It is the motivation that underpins all achievement, and when you manage it properly, you can use it to assist the healing process and prevent disease. So the key to stress management is—

perception ⟶ transformation

Moving from perception A to perception B means looking at things differently, a new interpretation which creates the transformation from powerless to powerful.

But before we get into ways to combat unhealthy stress . . .

I want to emphasize that stress is the result of subtle or not so subtle micro- and macrostressors. Examples of microstressors may be a low-volume but constant background noise, constant little irritations, stagnant or unhappy relationships, or ongoing, never-resolved problems at your place of employment. Microstressors tend to keep things stirred up but are not personally earth shaking in nature. They include worry, tension, and annoyances. Macrostressors, on the other hand, stand up and grab your attention, and they include devastating events such as death, divorce, being fired, or situations such as poverty, bankruptcy, an impossible-to-please boss, or traumas such as illness, drug abuse, moving, or the end of a romance. Managing our stressors is paramount to good mental health. Please make a list of your stressors. For example, write down your three stressors in each of the following three categories and decide if they are micro- (small) or macro- (major) stressors:

Home and Family

1. _____

2. _____

3. _____

Professional or Job Related

1. _____

2. _____

3. _____

Personal and Relationships

1. _____

2. _____

3. _____

The following is a technique that is called "the ACT formula" and was created by Gary Emery, Ph.D., and James Campbell, M.D.[11] Their book, *Rapid Relief from Emotional Distress,* is an excellent companion resource to therapy.

The ACT Formula
I will accept my current reality.
I will choose what I can do about it and then visualize it.
I will take action.

Suppose that you wrote under your list of stressors something like these responses:

Home and Family
My spouse is an alcoholic and won't get help.   **Macro**

Professional or Job Related
My boss is on me all the time.   **Macro**

Personal and Relationships
I have no one that I can really talk to.   **Macro**

Putting the ACT formula to use, your new statements would look like this:

- I accept that my husband is an alcoholic.
- I choose to take care of myself and can visualize my life being happier.
- I will take action by joining a support group and filing for divorce.

- I accept that my boss is on me all of the time.
- I choose not to allow his behavior to affect my emotions and can visualize a more calm atmosphere.
- I will take action by telling him my limits and, if necessary, look for another job.

- I accept that I have no one to talk to about problems.
- I choose to change that and can visualize friendships.
- I take action by joining a club, trying to be more friendly by inviting people over to my home.

One of the things that I often see patients doing to themselves is using negative self-talk, often repeating what they heard as a child from their parents or from others in their lives. This pattern can be traced back to their *belief* about themselves that reinforces a negative self-concept. This ingrained behavior also greatly interferes with the ACT formula. Using our same examples, let me contrast the difference that positive self-talk can have on your choices.

My spouse is an alcoholic and won't get help.

Self-Talk	Negative:
A	It's my fault, I say too much.
C	If I were a better spouse, I could change and help him/her.
T	I can't leave because of finances and the kids.

Self-Talk	Positive:
A	I am responsible for my own behavior, no one else's. I am not helpless.
C	I can make good decisions. I can choose a better way.
T	I'll take action by looking into support groups for myself, community resources, and so on.

My boss is on me all of the time.

Self-Talk	Negative:
A	I deserve to be yelled at. I probably do make lots of mistakes.
C	I'm a loser. This is the only job I can get. I need the money.
T	I'll just have to put up with it.

Self-Talk	Positive:
A	I am responsible for my own behavior, no one else's. I am not helpless.
C	I can make good decisions. I can choose a better way.
T	I'll take action by looking into different job possibilities.

I have no one that I can really talk to.

Self-Talk	Negative:
A	I know that I am not very interesting. Who would want to be my friend?
C	You can't trust people anyway. I can just imagine that if I told someone what I really felt, they would tell others and laugh at me.
T	That's just my lot in life.

Self-Talk	Positive:
A	I am a good person and am capable of being a good friend.
C	I can choose to be a bit friendlier and put forth more of an effort.
T	I can see my life being happier when I take action to join a club or church.

Now that you have both techniques, rewrite your list of stressors, applying the ACT formula and using positive self-talk.

Home and Family Stressor

STATEMENT OF STRESSOR: _____

_____

Positive Self-Talk

A _____

C _____

T _____

Professional or Job Related

STATEMENT OF STRESSOR: _____

_____

Positive Self-Talk

A _____

C _____

T _____

Personal and Relationships

STATEMENT OF STRESSOR: _____

_____

Positive Self-Talk

A _____

C _____

T _____

Everyone has stress—it is a natural part of life—but you must make a decision about whether you control stress or whether stress controls you.

If the latter is the case, then disease can set in. Learning how to take control of your stress will help you relieve tension, help you cope with the unknown, and help put balance in your life.

I want to contrast the differences between stress and depression . . .

I often think these differences become confused in our label-happy society. Some of the symptoms of depression seem to overlap stress symptoms. Stress in many ways can set the stage for a serious depression, and depression often is the by-product of stress—and so is burn-out. There are several types of depression, including one that seems to have a genetic or inherited component, but there is no doubt in my mind that stress can trigger an episode of depression. Stress often acts as a precursor to depression. Stress symptoms are warnings from our body signaling us to change course or slow down. Such messages should be heeded.

Remember, stress is the imbalance between perceived demands of a stressful event and the perceived response capabilities of the individual. Whether this imbalance is great or small results in differences in coping with the stress. If the imbalance is great, then the inability to cope begins the degeneration compromise of the immune system resulting in illness.

Perception of the Event—Crisis or Challenge?

Psychological Correlates to Disease	Symptoms of Stress	Symptoms of Depression
unresolved family-of-origin	headaches	lack of concentration
stoicism	anxiety, nervousness	low feelings of self-worth
self-destruction	feeling angry or hostile	"what-is-the-use" attitude
feelings of loss	muscle tension	thoughts of suicide
compliance	low performance	weight loss or gain
self-sacrificing	irritability	difficulty sleeping
denial of anger	forgetfulness	feeling angry
inability to show emotions	overloaded	overwhelmed
caretaker	gastro-intestinal problems	exhaustion

Please Note: *I think it is important for you to understand the differences between stress and depression. If you feel you are truly depressed, I want you to ask your family doctor to recommend further treatment, such as medication and therapy. You may need help beyond the scope of our sessions in this book.*

Personality has an effect on how you deal with stress . . .

Maybe you thought you could be immune to stress—no such luck! As a matter of fact your personality may very well affect how well you deal or do not deal with stress. Your personality development is influenced by your family of origin and your life experience.

Many people have studied personality, and, as a result, there are many theories regarding personality types. The one I like is a thumbnail sketch about personality that is described by Florenez Littauer in *Personality Plus*.[12] Basically, this shorthand theory says that there are four types of people in the world:

Sanguine	+	popular, loving, optimistic, funny, sociable, spirited talker
	–	disorganized, changeable, forgetful, undisciplined, show off, loud, wants credit
Choleric	+	confident, productive, achiever, competitive, strong willed, forceful leader
	–	controlling, bossy, impatient, nervy, domineering, intolerant, manipulative
Phlegmatic	+	diplomatic, considerate listener, peaceful, tolerant, adaptable, pleasant
	–	slow, worrier, unenthusiastic, plain, doubtful, indifferent, indecisive
Melancholy	+	analytical, thoughtful, planner, perfectionist, respectful, loyal
	–	insecure, resentful, critical, unforgiving, hard to please, moody

Now, as you probably have already noticed, there are positive (+) as well as negative (–) traits in each category. Can you identify your personality style? By the way, no one has to be strictly in one category or another; you can be a mixture. I want to reassure you that whichever category or categories that fit you best, each has potential and excellent de-stressing modifiers. Allow me now to point them out for each category.

Sanguine

The sanguine personality is quite likable, fun, and enjoyable to be around. The animated, playful nature of the sanguine helps them to diffuse stress through a sense of humor and cheerfulness. Sanguines, however, tend to be disorganized and undisciplined, and this creates stress. Sanguines need to pace themselves in order to help limit the stress they create through their unpredictable and undisciplined behavior. To lower your stress when married to or working for a sanguine,

(1) Smile and show emotion.
(2) Write things down and never assume they heard or understood you.
(3) Use their name and compliment them often.

Choleric

The strong-willed choleric, who is competitive, resourceful, and self-reliant, tends to diffuse stress quite easily through a strong-willed style. Cholerics seem to thrive on stress but can be helped to avoid stress overload through verbal expression (channeled appropriately) and physical exercise. In dealing with cholerics, you can reduce your stress level if you

(1) Anticipate their impulsiveness and abruptness (remember, it's not personal—it's just how they behave).
(2) Present options in a brief fashion.
(3) Lower your voice when speaking to them.

Phlegmatic

The phlegmatic is a rather peace-loving, shy, and reserved individual who needs to be encouraged to express feelings of doubt and worry. Because they tend to be timid and slow, they can air out feelings of anger through physical exercise. Pets are great stress relievers for phlegmatics and so are books and soothing music. When involved with a phlegmatic, to reduce your stress level

(1) Be very reassuring and try to minimize conflict.
(2) Anticipate their desire for perfection.
(3) Compliment them for any positive changes or accomplishments.
(4) Be very cautious about kidding around or teasing them.

Melancholy

The melancholy who is very sensitive, orderly, thoughtful, and insecure can easily become depressed and introverted. Melancholies need to avoid employers who tend to be choleric. While relief through meditation is excellent for all personality types, it is especially beneficial for a melancholy. When involved with melancholies, to reduce your stress

(1) Prepare them ahead of time for any change.
(2) Be respectful of their routines, schedules, and slowness.
(3) Try to explain how you feel and any reasons you may have for wanting things to change.

We can now work together to find some relief for your stressors . . .

The foundation for any stress-management program is to learn first how to relax. In the back of this book I have included my personal deep muscle relaxation technique that I want you to use at least one time each day. I also want to teach you a few "minirelaxers" to be used during the day, especially during difficult periods.

Minirelaxers

Suppose that you have written under Professional or Job Related stressors that a certain coworker or boss gives you a difficult time. Picture in your mind this stressful image for thirty to forty seconds. Be aware of the beginning of any tension in your body, any sense of anxiety. As the bad feeling subsides, begin to take a few deep breaths and then make your shoulders and eyebrows relax. Take two more deep breaths and repeat the process until you have effectively diffused or de-stressed the formerly stressful image.

The more you practice this technique, the more proficient you will become. You will be gaining a sense of control over the stressful situation, a state of mind that is an automatic de-stressor.

The most common reason people feel stressed is that they feel they have no control over the matter. The situation is either out of hand or they feel trapped and without any choice. You always have a choice. Admittedly, the choices may not appear to be good ones, but you do have a choice. Once you begin saying that message to yourself, you will start feeling in control. For instance, take the image you chose when I asked you in the preceding example to imagine a stressor from your job and ask yourself this question:

What can I do to change the situation?

If you cannot come up with a change, then you have two rational choices:

1. You must adapt to and accept the situation.
   or
2. You must find another job.

I encourage people to take risks, but I ask them to do so thoughtfully. If you hate your job and it causes you stress, please find another one! Life is too short to be stressed out and unhappy. If you are involved in a miserable relationship, again, do something different—accept things as they are or get out! From feeling trapped or feeling like a victim springs anger and turmoil—so take control! Find some peace and happiness. You deserve to be treated with kindness and respect. Don't settle for anything less. *Bad jobs and/or bad relationships = poor self-image.* Again, remember that you always have two choices:

1. You must adapt to and accept the situation.
   or
2. You can get out.

I am now going to discuss some concepts that deal with "faulty wiring"

. . .

Anyone participating in these sessions probably would agree that he or she has some degree of "faulty wiring." At the beginning of your life you learned a dysfunctional method that lends itself to manipulation through self-induced action—how you hear and see things (perception). So the goal here is to do some "rewiring." Any action you might deliberately choose from within your own psyche can become a tool, either positive or negative, that you can employ to help you change your behavior (rewiring). This rewiring takes place in what I call the *Interpretation Loop.* For example, your interpretation of an event or situation affects how you deal with it. What you say to yourself (in your thoughts) at the time of the event will determine how intense or stressed the situation becomes and what you will feel. How powerless or powerful you feel depends on your choices. There are three critical areas to be considered in the *Interpretation Loop*. They are:

1. **Prediction**—the thought that tells you what is going to happen.
2. **Evaluation**—the thought that tells you how well you are doing.
3. **Interpretation**—the thought that tells you what the other person is going to do.

Two other subcomponents complete our diagram. They are

1. **Physiological Reaction**

   Your autonomic system kicks in with

   a. shaky hands, sweaty palms, palpitations, light headedness
   or
   b. self-control

2. **Behavioral Reaction**

   a. lying, making excuses, running away
   or
   b. dealing with the problem.

So the Interpretation Loop looks like this:

Interpretation Loop

Event

Interpretation

Physiological Reaction
Behavioral Reaction

Prediction

Evaluation

The Prediction, Evaluation, and Interpretation (P-E-I) elements act as reinforcements to each other and escalate or deescalate the Physiological and Behavioral Reactions (P_R, B_R). The sum of the parts determine your power (P):

$$\frac{P}{I} = (P_R + B_R) = P \pm$$

In any communication, prediction, evaluation, and interpretation all occur. What sometimes seems to be missing are two very essential elements:

1. Checking out your data for accuracy = **Accuracy Mechanism**
2. Making a choice based on that data = **Choice Mechanism**

For example, if your spouse tells you that he or she is unhappy with how the marriage is going, your Interpretation Loop begins like this:

Prediction—This is going to lead to a fight. (*What is going to happen.*)
Evaluation—I am a lousy spouse. (*How you are doing.*)
Interpretation—She is going to leave me. (*What he or she is going to do.*)

Physiological Reaction—Your mouth may be dry, and you feel nervous.
    Choice Accuracy: You remain calm and repeat back what your spouse said.

Behavioral Reaction—You feel defensive and start making excuses.
    Choice Accuracy: You deal with the problem after looking at options together and asking questions for further clarification.

But if you add accuracy and choice to the loop, things begin to change. You understand clearly what is being said even if your spouse must repeat it several times. We call this active listening, and the process goes like this: Partner A states his or her position and feelings to Partner B. Next, Partner B tells Partner A what he or she has heard. If Partner A does not feel that Partner B understands what was said, Partner A repeats it. Then Partner B again states what he or she heard. You do this until Partner A is satisfied that Partner B really understands the point. Then it is Partner B's turn to state his or her position and feelings using the same method. Although this may seem cumbersome at first, stick with it because it really clarifies communication. Hence, the *Accuracy Mechanism.*

Next, you ask questions to gather facts. Anytime you are making a decision or exercising choice, the more data that you have, the better the decision or choice. In Session 8, we will discuss the role of Defense Mechanisms—the ways in which we protect ourselves. But good communication is promoted by openness, and I will teach you some techniques that encourage supportive communication. When you combine what you are learning now with Session 8, your Interpretation Loop will be even more empowered. Hence, the *Choice Mechanism.*

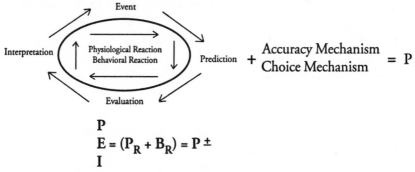

$$\frac{P}{I} \quad E = (P_R + B_R) = P \pm$$

With the addition of the Accuracy and Choice Mechanisms, the prediction, evaluation, and interpretation become more positively oriented and clear. This addition allows you to say, "Okay, a mistake was made, but that happens, and it is not the end of the world." Most people are reasonable and will work with you. If they are not and you have done all you can, remember that you are in control and can make wise decisions. Your *Interpretation Loop* is now complete and is at your command to help you sift through the negatives, to stop beating yourself up, and to allow you to make solid choices.

But how do you access the loop? You do so by making some lifestyle changes that promote self-love and allow the light to enter. Second, you polish your decision-making and choice techniques.

You should know about some very sound suggestions for changing behavior . . .

I call them *Light Promoters,* and they act as a filter to stress. As you will see, they clearly outline life-style changes as well as psychological changes:

- One of the main principles in stress management is to maintain a strong foundation by practicing *good health and fitness.* This certainly includes eating correctly and exercising regularly. *Proper rest* is important as well.

- *Becoming more aware of yourself and others* will help you identify early signs of stress. What kind of demands are on you and how are you handling them? Can you anticipate stressful events and begin early coping strategies?
- It is also very important to *take responsibility for your actions*—this helps you feel more in control and empowered. Remember that blame and excuses in the long run cause anger and pain and lead to feelings of being a victim.
- Look for *inner strength* through prayer or meditation. Those are two wonderful and effective ways to reduce stress.
- *Be kind to yourself* and *maintain patience* toward your imperfections and adversity. Focus on how far you have come!
- Another helpful de-stressor is through the maintenance of a *strong support system,* which may consist of your family and/or friends. Being able to express fear, anger, and frustration reduces emotional pressures and bonds you with others. A support system can provide warmth and encouragement and can give you other people's insights on stress management. Along these same lines these family members or friends can assist you in problem solving and decision making.
- The creation of a *personality stability zone* can go a long way toward de-stressing. Examples of such a zone might include a special chair, listening to or performing music, or even wearing an article of clothing such as an old bathrobe.
- The best de-stressor of all that I can think of is a *pet.* There has been much research in an area called psychoneuroimmunology, which is an extremely large word to describe the things we have just discussed. One of the strongest recommendations that comes out of this research is evidence of the benefits provided by pets. Many nursing homes are using pet therapy to help patients cope with anxiety and loneliness. A dog, cat, fish, bunny, or the like is a wonderful adjunct to any stress/de-stress program.

The Serenity Prayer

*God, grant me the serenity to accept the things
   I cannot change,
the courage to change the things I can,
and the wisdom to know the difference.*
                                        Author unknown

Session 8 _____

Defense

_____

Issues we will cover in Session 8:

- **Skewed needs** — Intrusions from our past, left unsettled, can program you for destructive behaviors and illness.
- **Defense mechanisms** — In troubled families you learn ways to protect yourself.
- **Poisonous voices** — Your head may be filled with fears generated by this cancerous internal voice, which you can combat by "reframing" with the truth.
- **Four fears** — The four major categories of fear are rejection, anger, trauma, and failure (or success), and at least one or more of these may be keeping you in bondage.
- **Reparenting** — Learn how fear relates to old beliefs, events, goals, and old truths, and change them into new truths and new results.

In Session 7 we discussed stress and its positive and negative effects on your life. Through some stress-management techniques, I helped you learn ways to put stress to work for you. Using positive self-talk through the ACT formula was one technique you are now using that I hope will be helpful. Also, I hope you know the difference now between symptoms of stress and symptoms of depression.

As an adult you may find yourself mired in pain from your turbulent childhood . . .

This pain means you are probably still hearing that inner parental voice that nags you into believing you are bad, unworthy, stupid, shamed, and unlovable. This same intrusion programs you for failure, bad relationships, destructive behaviors—doom and gloom. Because things were so totally out of control in your early life, because children have no power and must do as they are told, and because their innocence is abused and misused, the needs that went unmet become distortions of good mental health. And so these skewed needs look like this:

> The need to have power over others
> The need to manipulate others
> The need to be angry, critical, judgmental
> The need to be a victim
> The need to be codependent or caretaking

What's really happening here is that you are looking in the mirror and seeing or hearing that poisonous parent. As if things weren't bad enough, we reinforce these messages with actions that support the poison. Most of the time people are not even aware they are being controlling, judgmental, angry, thoughtless, smothering, demanding, wimpy, or helpless. The realization usually comes when they have failed relationships, disappointing careers, no friends, and become miserable and unhappy folks.

But you are a survivor and you have learned various ways to protect yourself...

We call these protective behaviors defense mechanisms because defending us is their purpose. It is a way of hiding from the world—first by avoidance and second by attack. These mechanisms are unconscious habits that distort reality, and although they do offer you protection, the price is surviving—not living.

Defense Mechanisms

Rationalization — Unconscious justification of a behavior by reasons or motives other than the truth.
  Example: I deserved to be beaten because I was bad, or I drink a lot because I am under so much stress.

Reaction formation — Unconsciously not facing a problem by acting in a way that is the extreme opposite.
Example: Many "activists" become immersed in a cause (like anti-pornography or fanatic religiosity) to repress their actual, unacceptable attitudes and desires.

Projection — Placing on others an unpleasant or unacceptable trait of your own in order to escape your own truth.
Example: Complaining that "the boss is unfair" or "your spouse is lazy" when actually those descriptions belong to you.

Repression — Painful experiences leave the consciousness and become buried deeply in the unconscious.
Example: An abused child who as an adult has no memory of what happened to her. Or, someone who has witnessed trauma, such as a Vietnam veteran, but who has no conscious recall of the event.

Dependency or regression — Unconsciously retreating to a less mature or younger state and using this helplessness to maintain your integrity.
Example: I would really like to get better, but I just can't. Rather than admitting that you don't want to try, you say "I can't."

Emotional insulation — Rather than risking pain, one becomes aloof and emotionally remote and unavailable.
Example: Someone hurts you in a relationship or in childhood so you opt to reduce your emotional involvement.

Denial — The blotting out of the part of reality that threatens your self-esteem by ignoring that reality or overlooking it.
Example: Sometimes parents will deny any or all incidents of abusing their children, or an alcoholic will label his or her drinking as "social."

Acting out — The attempt to reduce the tension of inappropriate impulses by giving them quick, direct expression.
Example: People act out their feelings with an act of violence, by destruction of property, through sex (infidelity or promiscuity), or with verbal assaults.

Displacement — Unconscious substitution of a nonthreatening situation in place of a threatening one.

Example: A person gets "chewed out" by the boss, but because he does not want to risk his employment, he takes out his anger and hostility on an animal, object, or a defenseless spouse or child.

Intellectualization — The use of a rational explanation to insulate oneself from the negative, emotional feelings that would normally accompany the event.

Example: In this situation you dispassionately take a rather detached look at an event, such as loss of a loved one, and explain (sometimes in great detail) what happened without feeling it.

Certainly, this is not a complete list of defense mechanisms, but these are definitely the most popular!

1. What defense mechanisms do you use to protect your self-image? List each with examples.
2. What were you protecting?
3. What were the consequences of these defenses?
4. How could you have done things differently?

Many people spend a great deal of time and energy using defense mechanisms . . .

We already agreed that they were developed in order to help you survive at the expense of truly living. Being defensive creates a self-imposed isolation. It puts others off and prevents the very thing most needed—love and acceptance. You probably now have a good grasp about why you are defensive, and this means two things:

1. You are growing.
2. You are ready to make some changes!

Dr. Jack Gibb[13] researched and identified six defensive behaviors, but his greatest contribution came with the development of six contrasting supportive behaviors. He theorized that defensiveness was reciprocal, but so is supportiveness. Gibb explained that defensive behavior begets defensive behavior, but supportive behaviors can neutralize the defenses because supportive behavior reduces the fear.

The Gibb Categories of Defensive and Supportive Behaviors:

Evaluation vs. Description

If you want to escalate defensive behavior, use the language of "evaluation" or judgment. Examples of evaluation often begin with "you" (or "you" appears somewhere in the statement) such as

> *You* are so sloppy.
> *You* are so stupid.
> *You* would lose your head if it weren't attached.
> When are *you* going to become responsible?

There is now a massive need on the part of the receiver to protect his or her self-concept, which often means a counterattack will be launched.

The defuser or supportive behavior is "description" and usually begins with "I-language," a method described by Thomas Gordon. Instead of judging, you merely describe how the behavior affects you. So,

> "You are so sloppy" becomes "I feel uncomfortable when things are out of place. How can we change things?"
> *or*
> "You would lose your head if it weren't attached" becomes "I feel frustrated when things are out of place. Maybe we could decide on a special place for keys and things."

Control vs. Problem Orientation

When people send you a message that clearly implies that they have their minds made up without further discussion, you feel discounted and angry. People control others in various ways, such as with words, tone of voice, gestures, status, physical power, or money. In essence, their message is, "It's my way or the highway!"

So the supportive behavior for control is problem orientation. The attitude expressed is one of a willingness to share in decision making, problem solving, and compromise.

"And this is how it will be done" becomes "Let's find an answer that works for both of us."

This approach shows mutual respect and consideration.

Strategy vs. Spontaneity

"Strategy" is another word to describe "manipulation." This is a favorite tactic of con-artists and leaves the victim feeling used or tricked. To strategize is to plot, and this usually evokes anger. Example,

> Suppose you want to go to a store that is having a great sale, but you do not have a car. So you call a friend and tell her about all these bargains and that you just knew she would love to know about it. "Even though I really don't have the time to go," you say, "as a special favor I will rearrange my schedule for you. Pick me up in half an hour!"

Gibb says that a better way to do this is to be spontaneously honest. Just plainly ask in a direct fashion for what you want.

> So you call your friend and say, "I know it's short notice, but if you don't have other plans, there is a terrific sale going on. My car is in the shop, so you would have to drive."

Neutrality vs. Empathy

No one likes to feel insignificant, and neutrality or indifference conveys just that. The sender, often through body language, evokes feelings of "I am not important." People who are aloof and detached inspire others to be defensive. An example might be the spouse who pours out her heart about something she feels is important and gets a response of "pass the salt." The indifferent spouse may wind up with dinner in his lap!

The supportive behavior—empathy—means responding to what the sender is feeling. You don't have to agree; just be respectful.

> Your spouse comes home and tells you that she has had "the day from hell" at work. Her head is splitting from a headache, the boss chewed her out, and on the way home she had a flat tire! You respond by say-

ing, "I'm sorry, honey. It really does sound like a day from hell. Can I do anything?"

Superiority vs. Equality

When I was an undergraduate, I had an obnoxious professor who constantly reminded us of his extreme intelligence and superiority. But this professor had a bad habit of lecturing with a cigarette between two fingers and a piece of chalk next to it. His loftiness and superiority aroused feelings of inferiority in his students, so I found myself fantasizing about how great it would be if just once he would get confused and "take a drag" off the chalk. We all suffered through his grandiosity for an entire semester, and just when I thought that my fantasy was indeed dashed, the miracle happened. The poor guy nearly choked to death, and the entire class gave him a standing ovation! It was the highlight of the semester.

A red flag pops up whenever we feel that people are behaving in a superior way. This behavior is insulting and, at the same time, promotes their self-concept at our expense. Obviously, we all recognize that some people do sometimes possess an ability or talent or skill that is greater than ours, but people who act respectfully toward others—acknowledging that others also have specialness and equality—earn a reciprocal respect.

Certainty vs. Provisionalism

This is the last of Gibbs's categories. Folks who "know it all," who are absolutely certain that their way of thinking is the only way of thinking, are certainly obnoxious to others. (There is an old saying—"Do you want to have a relationship, or do you want to be right?") They basically are saying, "I know more than you and I'm going to prove it!" These people are only interested in being correct, and that is because deep down they fear being wrong. Their insecurities stick out all over the place, and they are a nightmare to deal with. People around them feel bullied and abused. Sadly enough, these very "certain" individuals have no idea how their behavior affects others. They are often lonely and angry and have few friends.

By using provisionalism, you allow others the right to their own opinions, and you can disagree respectfully. You utilize "I-language":

I think this way because . . .
I feel this is right because . . .

And you accept the idea that others have valid ideas and feelings. You avoid words of generalization such as "always," "everybody," "never," and instead say, "sometimes," "some people," "perhaps," "it seems."

Provisionalism promotes an openness to receive new ideas, beliefs, and information. When you respond in a supportive fashion, you create an atmosphere that is safe and secure—the basis for all good communication. It is extremely difficult and unpleasant to deal with a hostile and defensive individual. Such persons are so focused on not being hurt and protecting their self-image that they lose sight of what is really transpiring. The way to avoid this unpleasantness is

1. to become aware of how you may at times be defensive;
2. to change those defensive behaviors into supportive ones.

Our behavior is consistent with our self-concept . . .

If you feel that you are a "bad" person, then you will behave accordingly. Now is a good time to review your beliefs and value systems, as well as previous self-concept work. When you look at some of your "old" beliefs, take a look at who's talking! One way to put the negative voice in your head out of business is to track down that "criminal" and begin to recognize how fear influences those cancerous thoughts.

Fear may be described as an emotional as well as physiological response (just ask anyone who suffers from panic disorder!) to anticipated or perceived impending disaster. Its genesis may date back to childhood when you may have experienced neglect, absence of love, and other forms of abuse. Certainly any traumatic incident at any age has the same effect. That cancerous voice in your mind triggers the old "fight-or-flight" mechanism and becomes an obstacle to love.

There are four categories of fears:

Fear of rejection/abandonment
Fear of anger

Fear as a result of trauma
Fear of failure or of success

You are ready to harness your fears . . .

You can deal with your fears now based on what you have learned about yourself thus far, through your genogram, family history, and beliefs, but before we begin I do want to put in a "good word" for fear. Much like physical pain reminding us that something is wrong and that we need to see a physician, fear has a similar component. It also acts as a messenger, reminding us of something that haunts us from the past.

I treated an attractive young woman who was well educated, married, and had a successful career. Some might describe "Mary" as having it all. But beneath her strong, confident, happy-go-lucky veneer, she was plagued by nightmares and bouts of sheer terror. Her fears had begun to interfere with her marriage and career, so she came for some help. She had absolutely no recollection of any violence in her life, no accidents or near-death experiences. Yet all of her symptoms seemed to suggest a post-traumatic stress disorder. Mary was convinced that someone was going to kill her. Although she had lived with fear and anxiety for years, her symptoms worsened about two months prior to treatment, and she was at a loss trying to identify any triggering action. Her feelings were so severe that she wanted to die to stop the pain.

After much digging and probing during her hospitalization, it turned out that Mary had witnessed a gang murder when she was just a child in the seventh grade. She never told anyone—not even her parents—because of fear of retaliation. She had successfully repressed the incident all these years. Like many victims of violence, it was essential to Mary that she prove this unbelievable story had actually happened. Fortunately, she was able to do just that through a journalist friend who researched the events and finally managed to produce an old newspaper account that matched facts about the school and the time of the incident.

Mary suffered from post-traumatic stress disorder, a not uncommon emotional problem. This phenomenon is seen often in soldiers who come back from war and suffer from flashbacks or memories that are associated with trauma and atrocities. These events can be very crippling and spill over into daily life causing immobilizing fear, depression, anger, and self-sabotage. Your home burning down, a rape or kidnapping, an auto accident are examples of events that can cause post-traumatic stress disorder. To diffuse the disabling impact of these tragedies, it is necessary to identify them and then write and discuss every detail of the ordeal. Some of you may not even be aware of the cost of these situations, but dealing with them can be freeing.

Mary's fear of anger and reprisal almost cost her life because she had decided that she would kill herself before someone else did it. In therapy she was able to identify and discuss her fears and relate the pervasiveness of the pain from the trauma to other parts of her life and behavior. Her relief has freed her from the fear and pain and has allowed her to see herself differently—as a strong survivor.

So, now it's your turn . . .

Your fears may not be related to a specific incident like Mary's, but the process is the same. One of those four fears keeps you in bondage, but by tracing that fear, you can overcome it. This bondage is experienced through

Insecurity and Loneliness	→	Fear of rejection/abandonment
Uncertainty Hypervigilance Frustration	→	Fear of trauma
Resentment	→	Fear of anger
Emptiness and Meaninglessness	→	Fear of failure or success

1. Write down your earliest recollection of any fear.

2. Describe any other fearful events you have experienced.

3. How did you feel when things were going on?

4. Keeping in mind the four major causes of fear (rejection/abandonment, anger, trauma, success/failure), connect those past events to how you react today.

   List the fears: How I act:

5. Go back and "reframe" what happened. (Example: When we use the term reframe, we are asking you to see the positive aspect of the event. Mary felt helpless and terrified, but she reframed the event by replacing her old feelings with healthy, strong ones—and became a survivor. She was able to recognize that it took personal strength and courage to deal with such a sight but that she was capable of calling upon her coping strategies. After discussing it in detail, which diffused it in her mind, she consciously made an effort to replace the frightening thoughts with feelings of personal empowerment and thus prevailed.)

6. Rewrite the event and tell yourself the "truth." (Example: Yes, this incident was painful and horrible, but I have learned that I was not responsible and could do nothing to change what happened. I have decided to do some volunteer work with gang members in an effort to prevent such tragedies.) Repeat and repeat your new empowered truth!

Doing what parents should have done is another aspect of reparenting yourself . . .

Begin to reparent yourself by looking at your goals and beliefs in order to combat your fears. Part of the reason we don't accomplish what we want is because of fear. So, let's expand upon the process we just finished and learn how fear and its origin relate to our old beliefs, goals, and new truths.

Mary's Example:

Old Beliefs	Fearful Events	Goals	Old Truths
Someone is going to kill me.	Witnessed gang murder	Happy marriage	Fear of anger keeps me from telling my husband how I feel and blocks resolution of that anger.

Mary's Example:

New Truths	New Results
I am strong and can survive.	I can express my feelings and anger to my husband and allow him to express appropriately his feelings and anger also.

In the last two exercises you have learned how to rewrite or rescript the past—seeking the truth—and you have done something called "reframing" (how to see the results of fear, or any negative event, positively). So your new messenger (*also known as* fear) has become an ally. It's a wake-up call—a call to arms!—a call to truth!!

One other technique that you have picked up in the first exercise on fear has to do with self-messages. Remember when Mary "reframed" her "terror" by seeing that the real truth is that she overcame her terror with "strength through honesty." She changed terror to strength. Next, she rescripted the event and repeated to herself over and over, "I have learned I am strong and that I am a survivor." Out loud or silently, that healthy self-talk becomes another useful tool. When you hear that poisonous parent telling you that you are bad, dirty, or dumb, immediately affirm the truth.

> Example: I am a good person and lovable.
>
> I am kind and worthwhile.
>
> I am intelligent and a part of my creator.

Make a list of affirmations and say them regularly. Sometimes it's helpful to wear a lightweight rubber band on your wrist, and every time you hear the "lies," give yourself a little twitch with the rubber band and immediately correct the lie with an affirmation. It takes some time and practice to rid yourself of that critical parent. Their lies are deeply imbedded memories—but not cemented!

Understanding where fear comes from overcomes it!

Shame, Guilt, and Self-Sabotage

Issues we will cover in Session 9:

- **Love as conditional or unconditional** — The quality of love experienced in childhood can create a lifetime of trouble.
- **Shame and guilt** — These feelings are hidden behind emotional illness.
- **Addictions, abuse, and conditional love** — These dysfunctions create shame-based people.
- **Detoxification** — You have the power to detoxify your shame.
- **Boundaries** — Have you been allowed to develop healthy boundaries or forced to build desperate bunkers?

We have already come quite a distance together, but there are still miles to go. Please make certain that you have done the exercises thus far because they are your building blocks. In the last session we discussed fear. You discovered that you may have learned to protect yourself in childhood through defense mechanisms, and that while these defenses helped you survive, they do not enhance living. You then contrasted those defense mechanisms with supportive behaviors that help reduce fear. Finally, Session 8 taught you ways to reparent yourself and gave you some affirmations to help you control fear. In this session we are going to be discussing shame and guilt, all too common feelings that are hidden behind emotional illness.

Dr. Sigmund Freud laid the groundwork to help people understand and treat emotional disorders by providing us with a description of the self

. . .

Although much of his work has been challenged, Freud's[14] description of the self is still invaluable to the mental health profession. Freud hypothesized that the self is divided into three parts: the id, ego, and superego. He said that the *id* was our primitive side, always asking for more of everything, much like a demanding child. The *superego* is our conscience, the part that tells us right from wrong. Finally, the *ego* is the arbiter, the site of the battles that constantly occur between the id and the superego.

Superego
Ego   Self
Id

To illustrate the relationship, suppose you would like a second helping of chocolate cake. The id would applaud your decision despite the fact that you are overweight. The superego would be telling you that it would be wrong, bad for your health, and not to indulge. The ego would make the choice.

But the self can also be viewed as built from a higher self (superego) and a lower self (id and ego):

Higher Self =   Spiritual   =   Health
                     Love
                     Sixth Sense

                     Body, Personality
Lower Self =   Fear   =   Cancers of the Self
                     Guilt
                     Shame

Love can be given (or perceived) as being conditional or unconditional. Let me explain . . .

The lower self causes havoc because it functions out of fear, which is the opposite of love. In relationships, the lower self's idea of love is conditional. This self gives in order to get and demands qualifiers—"If you love me, you will lose weight; if you love me, you will never forget my birthday; if you love me, you will always behave." When this kind of conditional love is experienced in childhood, the framework for shame and guilt is established. Then, in adulthood shame-based people seek out one another and develop what is called a love/hate relationship. Because they were not nurtured and given unconditional love as children, they seek it from others and then wonder why relationships don't work for them.

The higher self is able to show love that is unconditional. Unconditional love comes from healthy people, who, unlike the lower self, have no hidden agenda attached to their love. This is love that is accepting and nondemanding and based on trust—"I love you no matter what!" Unfortunately, the divorce rate seems to suggest that few of us have achieved higher self-love. What I can tell you, though, is that by healing the cancer of the self and being committed to the psychotherapy in our sessions, you can move into that higher-self state.

Is conditional love ever healthy? Surprisingly, yes. If you are from a dysfunctional family that revolved around conditional love, you felt abused and hurt and less than normal as a result, and healing is necessary. After you have gone through these sessions, you can "choose" to love unconditionally your parents and others who have hurt you because they were your parents or someone important in your life. You can separate their *actions* from their *selves* and unconditionally love that part. But at the same time, you may use conditional love or "boundaries" that keep you safe. For example,

> Joe's father is manipulative and controlling, which limited and caused pain to Joe as a child. As an adult, still enmeshed in his father's behavior, Joe may unconditionally love his dad but through therapy resolve that it is too painful to be around his father and fall into the victim trap. It is Joe's father's decision to continue his illness, and Joe's decision to detach himself by no longer visiting him. As an adult, Joe is able to separate the two.

Parents who gave their children conditional love ("make me proud of you!") were incapable of seeing their children as separate from themselves. When they would look at their child, it was as if they were looking in the mirror at themselves. If the reflection was positive, love followed. If the reflection was negative, withdrawal of love or another form of abuse followed. This led the way to their child's feelings of guilt and inadequacy. From the child's fear of losing love, shame emerged! In effect, the child began to disown parts of himself in order to cope with the conditional love.

As adults, they become involved in destructive relationships where the conditional love or disowned parts become the attraction. So, women who are nurturing seek emotionally remote men (the conditional love established by the parent). Men who are kind and loving seek narcissistic (selfish) women. *Rule of thumb:* You marry the parent (someone like that parent) with whom you have the most difficulty. It is an effort (unconscious) to make right that primary relationship. To check this out, make a list of the qualities and behavior that your problem parent has. Now make a list of your spouse's or significant other's qualities and behavior.

Qualities of your problem parent:	Qualities of your spouse:
1.	
2.	
3.	
4.	
5.	
6.	
7.	
8.	
9.	
10.	

You have often heard the term that opposites attract, but all too frequently the attraction is pathological—the unfinished business of childhood.

One of the most obvious ways this drama was acted out was seen in the Broadway play and TV series *The Odd Couple.* Felix, the persnickety and fastidious perfectionist without taste or manners, shared an apartment with Oscar, the slob from hell. While Oscar's antics and uncouthness made Felix climb the wall, his freedom was often envied by Felix. Of course, the reverse was true for Oscar. They each represented the "disowned" parts from their childhoods—produced by the conditional love from parents—and the resulting adult behavior. *The Odd Couple* was funny to watch because in one way or another we all relate to those extremes. The success of the program, however, was owing to the absence of intimacy between these characters. These were two guys who shared an apartment. Their identities were never confused or entwined. But in an intimate relationship where there is a high degree of personal investment, the story is quite different.

Not only do we often enter intimate relationships in an attempt (unconscious) to work out the dysfunctional relationship we had with a parent or parents, but also we are saying to the world, this is the person I chose! He or she is part of my identity. The result is that when good old so-and-so screws up, that disowned part of the self triggers judgment, and so shame and rage build logarithmically with their behavior. Enter the parent you have married! The key here is to begin to make a conscious effort to define the disowned parts of the self, and then to begin to love yourself unconditionally. No one can do this for you. You cannot expect another person to fill your void—only you can fill it.

When you peel away the outer layers of guilt and shame, you find fear at their core . . .

Both guilt and shame can be healthy emotions, but before we look at the benefits, let's define the two and see the differences between them.

HEALTHY

Guilt	Shame
Guilt is a healthy part of our higher self. It is the emotional core of the superego and on a developmental stage begins around age three. It is felt when we digress from our beliefs and values.	Shame develops about the age of fifteen months.
	Healthy shame allows us to understand that we need help and that we need others.
Guilt does not reflect directly on one's worth or identity. It demands accountability and helps to establish boundaries.	Shame usually belongs to another person but we accept it for ourselves. For example, a child who

Guilt is a feeling of self-punishment that follows our belief that we have done something wrong.

was sexually abused grows up to feel the shame of this dreadful act because he or she is unable to see that the shame belongs to the perpetrator.

UNHEALTHY

Guilt

Guilt is the product of unhealthy parenting that demands perfectionism and conditional love. People with guilt often behave in a serious fashion and are plagued by unrealistic expectations of themselves. They assume responsibility for others' actions and see certain consequences as being their fault. Often they are martyrs and caretakers.

Shame

People feel powerless, worthless, hopeless, and helpless.

They have a pervasive sense of emptiness, self-doubt, and despair.

Their shame generates more shame and becomes the driving force behind cancers of the self.

These descriptions from John Bradshaw, who wrote *Healing the Shame that Binds You*,[15] illustrate the desperation that shame-based people feel. People often confuse guilt with shame because they use the word "guilt" or "guilt-ridden" when they really mean "shame." Shame is a very emotionally charged word because it describes the self and is internalized. Guilt, by contrast, is external and describes a reaction.

Most shame-based people come from families that have problems with addictions, abuse, conditional love, rage, or control . . .

Addictions may vary from alcoholism and drugs to workaholism, sex addiction, religiosity, eating disorders, rage obsessions, and control, but the common products of all addictions are hopelessness and worthlessness. Conditional love causes feelings of being fundamentally defective and thus breeds overreaction to even the smallest incident since it reminds us of a shame-inducing past event.

Rage uncovered is shame. It is a demeaning and fear-evoking emotion that strips a child or an adult of self-worth and confidence. Rage-aholics produce an atmosphere that suppresses the spirit and produces a chronic state of panic in which the individual must try to function. All energies are centered around survival and cause the absence of personal growth.

Control also suppresses the emergence of the spirit. Children who grow up with parents who are controlling often feel that they can do nothing right. They tiptoe through their childhood with a sense of meekness and dependency or with defiance and anger.

Go back and look over your genogram and personal history. Pay attention to what you were told about yourself and how your family contributed to your sense of shame.

What are the three most painful memories you have?

1.

2.

3.

What causes you to feel shame?

I once treated a young woman who was very shame based. Both parents were religious addicts. Sometime around four years of age a baby-sitter had performed oral sex on her. Sex was a taboo topic in her household, and it had been ingrained in her that sex was evil, dirty, and sick. Her early memory of such indoctrination was over an episode in which she was "caught" touching herself and was severely punished. Obviously out of fear, she never told her parents about the baby-sitter.

When she came to my office, she was shy and withdrawn and extremely depressed. My patient was about thirty years old, was married, and had two children. She had been treated for her depression many times but would always relapse. I put her in the hospital because she was suicidal. After some very intense therapy, she finally "confessed" that when she was about five or six, her family purchased a male dog, and she would allow, even encourage, the dog to lick her genitals.

Children who are sexually abused very often feel intense shame because, although they know it was wrong, sex did feel good. For some kids it was also the only time someone was "loving" toward them. It is a perverted type of love, but the child does not know that. Not all sexual abuse causes physical pain, and for some kids a feeling of "specialness" is promoted by the perpetrator. The child may enjoy gifts and special outings. But the price of this kind of love is the child's self-esteem. The abuse fosters the belief that the child is worthless and bad.

My patient's shame was so profound that she was willing to commit suicide rather than be exposed. Her life had been a nightmare of hiding, which she could bear no longer. Once her "crime" was out, she was reassured that she had done nothing wrong. After a lot more therapy, she was actually able to talk about her secret in a group. Members of the group further reassured her.

According to Bradshaw, people suffering from shame build a distorted belief system that in effect becomes a defense mechanism. Here are some examples. (Please remember that shame may have a variety of beginnings and is not limited to physical or sexual abuse.)

1. Shame-based people often hear the message that they are "oversensitive"—both verbal and nonverbal communications are "taken personally." All comments, gestures, words, and actions are somehow related to them personally.

   Problem "I saw the way he looked at me. He's mad!"
   "She didn't call me, so I guess she doesn't care."
   "My boyfriend says he wants to get away and go hunting.
   He really just wants to get away from me."

   Solution Stop jumping to conclusions—check things out through questioning.

2. Other shame-based thinking that is closely related to being "oversensitive" is "mind reading." In childhood you were given critical judgments about your value. As an adult you believe those judgments and believe that others agree with them.

   Problem "I know what he is thinking."
   "She said this, but really means this."
   "I'm going to assume he really wants this."

   Solution Take what people say at face value. Don't read things between the lines. Instead of "I know what he is thinking," use the word "fantasize." So . . . "I fantasize that this is what he is thinking." Then, ask questions!

3. Another form of shame-based thinking is "catastrophizing." This thinking is the result of insufficient boundaries. It is like the little child who keeps asking those "what if" questions but now drags those questions into adulthood.

> **Problem** "The sky is cloudy. I think it may rain, but what if the wind picks up. It's tornado season! And what would I do if a tornado hit? I would lose everything! If I lose everything, where will I go, and how will I rebuild what I had? I probably will become a street person with no home or food!" [And so on. . . .]

> **Solution** Ask yourself, what are the chances of this happening? Become aware of when you are beginning to escalate your interpretation of the situation and then go take a shower or call a friend. Break up the pattern. Don't indulge in creating fear.

4. And, then there is the "should, ought, and must" thinking. Its basis is a defense from childhood: Perfectionism = love.

> **Problem** "I *should* have done this, so that would not have happened."
> "I *ought* to be more generous."
> "I *must* stay late and get everything done."

> **Solution** I suggest to patients that they might ask themselves the question, "In terms of the entire universe, how important is this!?" Stop "should of-ing" yourself!

5. Shame-based thinking also includes "all or nothing" thinking. The message from toxic parents was, "If it's not perfect, it is no good and neither are you."

> **Problem** "I didn't make Johnny a good dinner last night; I am a terrible parent."
> "This is the way all things need to be done."

> **Solution** "All or nothing" thinking allows for no flexibility. You

don't give yourself any credit for your actions and interpret less-than-perfect behaviors from your significant
others as failure. Look for something you did do well.
Okay, so you didn't fix Johnny a good dinner. Did
Johnny go hungry? How about all of the other things you
do for Johnny?!

6. The "blame game" thinking is shame incognito. As a youngster you
were blamed for things beyond your control so you became defensive
and turned the tables. Blame is the first cousin to the defense-mecha-
nism rationalizations.

Problem   "I'm late because my wife forgot to set the alarm clock."
"I'm not being promoted because my boss is a jerk and
doesn't like me."
"I cheat on my wife because she doesn't understand me or
my needs."

Solution   Start taking responsibility for your behavior. Examine
how you contribute to problems. Do some self-nurtur-
ing.

**Guilt and shame have to express themselves somewhere, and one of the
most common ways is self-sabotage. . .**

In its less toxic form we call it procrastination—putting things off until
later. In its most toxic form it is rage and is usually turned inward, but it
can slip out given the right stimuli. Self-sabotage is like a thief that robs
you of your productivity, potential, and self-esteem, yet for many people it
is a chronic companion that may cause them to feel helpless and out of
control.

Self-sabotage comes in two forms—physical and emotional. The characteristics of *physical* self-sabotage include a variety of addictive behaviors
such as overeating, substance abuse, or inappropriate amounts of sleep
and no exercise.

The flip side is *emotional* sabotage. Such behaviors as procrastination,
anger, tardiness, lack of motivation, and rage are hallmarks of the problem. So how do you come to terms with these bandits:

1. Trace the genesis of your problem. Ask: How did I learn self-sabo-
    taging behaviors? Who taught me to avoid things?

    If you look closely, you will find that these behaviors never served
    your parents, mentors, or friends any better than they serve you.
    Quick escapes don't work!

    Remember that we never do anything without a "payoff" and that
    "payoffs" are not always positive. Self-sabotage keeps you from
    achieving your goals. Self-sabotage payoffs are always negative, but
    they do keep you stuck safely.

    First, list the ways in which you sabotage yourself and then next to
    it, the payoff—what you get out of it.

Physically	Payoffs
a. smoking	Become ill often and hope for pity.
b.	
c.	
d.	

Emotionally	Payoffs
a. unrealistic expectations	Never achieve, feel overwhelmed, and quit trying.
b.	
c.	
d.	

I told you about defense mechanisms in Session 8. Those most often
associated with self-sabotage are

> denial
> avoidance
> rationalization

2. Identify your defense mechanisms and ask yourself: What formulas do I use to set up my sabotage?

Example: Procrastinations → Defense Mechanism → Rationalization

Emotionally I make excuses such as, "I can do this later" or "I need to rotate my socks tonight."

Example: No exercise → Defense Mechanism → Denial

Physically "I am doing just fine. I am certain that my health is OK even though I have a family history of heart disease."

3. The language of self-sabotage is:
   "I can't" = dependency, helplessness
   "I should" = people pleasing
   "I have to" = control, caretaking

Over the next week try to be aware of how often you say these phrases. When you bring it all together, you are describing codependency, which is famous for creating anger in others!

4. Now let's look at these two specific areas and see how you have self-sabotaged them.
   A. relationship(s):
   B. career:

Until now your brain has been busily associating more pain with success than with failure, or more pain with health than with illness, but here's how to change that.

Recovery from Self-Sabotage — Taking Control

1. Describe how you would feel if you eliminated self-sabotage. Visualize the feeling and then write about it.

2. What would you gain? Visualize how different things would look and be, and then write about it.

3. Now, remember a time when you experienced success in spite of yourself, visualize it, and then describe it. Let yourself really feel how good and exhilarating it was. Feel the pride and confidence that accompanied that feeling. Write about it.

The next time you begin to slip into a sabotaging behavior immediately force yourself to feel what you felt when you were successful and act "as if" you have succeeded again. Your subconscious cannot tell the difference between what is real and what is not, so if you act "as if," you will be on your way to overcoming the negative behavior and replacing it with a positive one.

Let's look at other techniques. Remember my friend Shirley—Miss America with the crown? Essentially, what you are doing with the crown technique is changing your physiology. Its very difficult to self-sabotage when you are standing or sitting erect, smiling, making eye contact, acting "as if" you are enthusiastic (even if you have to fake it) , and gesturing in an animated fashion. Try it in front of a mirror and see and feel the difference!

Develop the habit of saying, "I want to," or "I choose to." It creates a mood of self-confidence and control. It flies in the face of feeling like a victim or dependent. Use positive self-talk frequently.

You don't have to be a victim of self-sabotaging thievery. Don't expect someone else to change your life situations. Free will allows *us* to change our own life situations. Empower yourself.

The way back from shame is to identify the shame-inducing event, and then to talk about it. . .

Once you stop hiding, the relief can be dramatic. Here are some principles for detoxification:

Detoxification
1. Come out of hiding.
2. Name or identify the event or problem.
3. Talk about it with a friend; remove its power over you.

People who have unhealthy guilt and shame have very few boundaries . . .

A boundary is a psychological concept that allows us to have a sense of who we are as separate individuals. Our thoughts are as separate as our feelings and emotions. Boundaries help to differentiate ourselves from others and help to protect us. When our boundaries are healthy, we know when we are being abused physically, psychologically, and emotionally and are able to stand up for ourselves and not allow others to violate us.

Children who grow up with a legacy of guilt and shame may have only a few boundaries or even sometimes *none!* Most of us are familiar with the phrase "my own space." This concept has to do with boundaries. Consider this illustration: If you are around someone who comes into your space, you suddenly feel intruded upon and take a step away. Unfortunately, sometimes in these situations you may find yourself "dancing" with this person because every time you move, so does he or she. The way to stop this is to say to that person, "I'm feeling uncomfortable, and I need an arm's length between us." Notice what was done here: You have a preconceived boundary that when violated makes you feel uneasy, so you reestablish your boundary by assertively reclaiming your space.

The most common experiences that cause physical boundaries to become blurred are physical violence, incest, neglect, toxic religiosity, and control . . .

Children who have endured these atrocities feel powerless to establish a boundary for themselves or set limits with others. They are often so needy for attention that they accept any attention, even when it's abusive. They confuse love with abuse. As adults, then, if they are not being abused, they may believe that they are not being loved. Again, we do what we know because that's what feels normal.

To determine the state of your boundary, ask yourself the following questions:

1. How do I feel when someone gets too close?
2. How do I feel when someone touches me?
3. How can I assertively tell them to stop?

Appropriate boundaries promote healthy relationships and love . . .

Emotional boundaries guard against your assuming responsibility for others' unhealthy behaviors and allow ownership of your own feelings. Children who were reared by parents who expected their child to take care of them, to make decisions, or to solve problems beyond their years or who were humiliated and shamed verbally don't build boundaries—they build bunkers. Families that have emotional entanglements or enmeshments (such as inappropriate touching, sex lectures, or not allowing their children to individuate and become their own persons by controlling them with money even into adult life) heighten the child's need for a bunker to protect himself or herself from a barrage of demanded beliefs and feelings that the entire family has assumed. In such families there is no freedom to develop individuality or to allow room for autonomy.

Bunkers are built out of fear . . .

A few sessions back I asked you to identify your feelings, and I even gave you some examples of feelings since I anticipated that perhaps you might have trouble identifying them on your own. The feelings that are most often associated with a lack of emotional boundaries are

> worthlessness
> mistrust
> trouble accepting or giving love
> denial of feelings of anger or rage
> aloofness
> shame

As an adult, you can see more fully why your love relationships have been problematic or perhaps even disastrous. Emotional bunkers are not the best atmosphere for romance, love, and commitment. I think it is time to tear down the bunker that closes you off from everything and build a boundary that provides choice, autonomy, and love. To establish healthy emotional boundaries, ask yourself the following questions:

1. Who triggered feelings that were the result of criticism, humiliation, entanglement, and caretaking?

2. Who in my present life sets off those same old feelings?

3. How can I protect myself?

Prescription for Change

First, recognize that you have a right to think, feel, and believe anything you wish.

Second, you can choose to stay away from toxic people.

Third, when someone triggers old feelings, tell them using "I" language. Example, "When this happens, I feel . . ."; "I choose to disagree with you because I . . ."; "I choose not to do . . ."; "I choose to do. . . ."

Fourth, use self-talk. For example, say to yourself: "Okay, I have just allowed someone to make light of my feelings [minimize the hurt] and now I have allowed shame to sneak in. I won't let this happen again." Or, "Just because someone disagrees with me doesn't devalue my thoughts or decisions."

Fifth, the way your family may have treated you engendered your self-doubt. Use the ACT Formula to check if what you are feeling is rational. Example:

"My parents want me to come home for the holidays. My family is toxic. There will be arguments, lectures, problems, and criticism. If I don't go, they will make me feel shame and everyone will be angry. But part of me really wants to go and spend the holidays with them."

A— Accept that your parents' and family's behavior won't change; it never has. (Rational)

C— Look at your options: (1) You can go and feel more ill; (2) you cannot go and choose not to feel guilty; or (3) you can go for one or two days, establishing your boundaries before the trip.

T— Take action and stick to it. Discuss it with a trusted friend if you are still not certain.

Sixth, because everyone is accustomed to "business as usual," understand that setting boundaries will take some adjustment for you and your family and friends. Saying "No" or "I won't" will not be words that are very welcomed. But you have to take care of you; trust me, no one else will! So accept that you will meet lots of resistance, but vow to stick to your guns. When loved ones complain that you have "changed," you will know that you are on the right track. Be assured that boundaries will not only help you, but others will benefit as you become less shamed and more loving.

Seventh, journal writing is another "therapy from the soul" (see Session 10). In essence you have been doing just that and more in each session we have together. Long after you have completed our sessions, continue to write on a daily basis your thoughts, feelings, joy, pain. I believe that journaling (as we say in the business) is a real short cut in therapy and one more way to touch our unconscious. A word of caution—keep your journal in a safe and private place. In this way you will be setting a boundary that protects you from intrusive others. Once you have begun your journaling, don't reread anything in it for three weeks; then, go back to it. You will be surprised with what surfaces. By now you have gained valuable knowledge about you and your family. You are also learning solid therapeutic tools that can change your life and heal the "cancer of the self." Going through the psychotherapy in these sessions will make your journal far more meaningful!

Eighth, Use the formula: When you . . . I feel . . . because . . .

Example:

> *When you* tease me about my weight, *I feel* embarrassed and angry *because* my self image feels attacked.
> *or*
> *When you* say I will never amount to anything, *I feel* very hurt *because* I am afraid you must not like me.
> *or*
> *When you* yell at me, *I feel* belittled and humiliated *because* it is like being a child.

I cannot leave this discussion of boundaries without addressing spiritual boundaries . . .

Patients will often tell me that they feel they are "nuts" or "crazy" because they have been living a life based on confusion and denial. They can't quite separate reality from "pretending that things are all right." From all outward appearances, life seems to be going well. They come from "successful" families (parents were pillars of society) and have a reasonable relationship with them. They married well (like their parents), have great careers or professions, and are personally attractive, well-educated people, financially secure (not always), and upwardly mobile.

One such young woman came to see me complaining of vague dissatisfaction, a sense of unhappiness and confusion about life. She did so with a bright smile, self-assurance, and with an "is-this-all-there-is" attitude. She also told me that she felt ashamed of herself for feeling that way because life had been so good. (Remember the rule "Don't be selfish.") Upon taking her family history, she told me that her father was a successful lawyer and by necessity worked long hours (a workaholic). Her mother was an accomplished artist and did charity work (unavailable). My patient had one brother whom she described as cold and intense but who would do anything for her (confusion) and was a computer expert.

Upon graduating from college, "Jane" (not her real name) embarked upon climbing the corporate ladder at a large company and was doing well. Along the way she met and married a young attorney who was busy building his practice. She was insightful enough to see that she had recreated her family of origin and after some work recognized that her mother essentially had "painted" her life for her, right down to the smile on Jane's face. Jane told me her problem in our first session—that she felt ashamed of herself. The genesis of that shame was emotional neglect, a lack of nurturing, and having life planned for her. Jane had little sense of self and had just been going along with the program. Jane's parents were certainly not bad, but they were overcontrolling, emotionally absent (because of problems engendered by *their* parents), and love was conditional (based on expectations). Jane's parents went through all the right parental motions, including taking her and her brother to church. Jane best describes her early religious beliefs as "If you do or don't do this or that, you will burn in hell." So she perceived God as another controlling and conditionally loving parent. Jane suffered an emotional void from her parents' conditional love and a spiritual void from her perception of God's conditional love.

Once Jane learned about spiritual boundaries, she began to feel less bound to her parents' beliefs and started thinking for herself. She read many books and attended a variety of religious groups. She gleaned information from all of this and began her own spiritual enlightenment. She also came to the essential understanding that while she loved her parents and husband, she could not expect them to meet her emotional needs; that was her own job. Jane made some other decisions. In order to feel more fulfilled, she quit her job and is back in school. This time she is doing what she wants to do—studying music therapy!

I believe that God is all-loving, merciful, and forgiving. He endowed us with the gift of free choice.

Your Spiritual Boundaries

- What do you believe about God? Or, what are your beliefs about a higher power? (Not what you were told—but what you think and feel.)

- Have your beliefs changed since childhood?
- Describe or draw how your higher power looks.
- When do you feel the presence of your God or this power?
- It is okay to be angry with God or your higher power. Describe this anger.
- What is your relationship with your creator?

Therapy from the Soul

Issues we will cover in Session 10:

- **Therapy from the soul** — Art, dreams, meditation, prayer
- **Guardian angels** — This spirit is within you.
- **The child spirit** — This concept is not "hokey" after all and, as a special part of the self, may just provide a direct pipeline to your emotional health.
- **The keeper of pain** — The child within you is burdened with all the pain and abuse accumulated from your past.
- **Reparenting** — These exercises can help you experience the unconditional love you missed.
- **Kelly's story** — Kelly's child spirit saved her life.
- **Metaphors for life** — These word tools help you see yourself differently.

In Session 9 you were able to look at the quality of love that you experienced as a child. Whether it was conditional or unconditional left you feeling free or shameful and guilty. We looked at self-sabotage and ways to stop it by establishing boundaries for yourself and others. In this session we will experience therapy from the soul, creative and loving ways to heal.

Therapy from your soul is available to you right now . . .

Inside each of us dwells our spirit, which connects us to a fundamental power—the source of all that is created and in existence. God has given us some very revealing and fascinating abilities that I refer to as "therapy from the soul." They include art therapy, dreams, guardian angels, child spirit, metaphors, and inner guidance through visualization, meditation, and prayer. I believe that these tools allow us to visit, talk with, and hear our creator's messages. Whether you believe in a supreme being does not matter, the tools still work! Some people may be more comfortable thinking of these tools as "intuition."

Artwork can be very enlightening even if you don't think of yourself as "artistic"...

The first of these gifts is art therapy—a very fascinating, nonthreatening experience. Through art, people have illustrated their fears and doubts, pain and joy, and this has allowed them to express what they are unable to just say. Even the most articulate of us sometimes is at a loss for words to describe deep thoughts and feelings, so drawings let our inner self be heard.

I once treated a very intelligent man who had experienced a tragic childhood and was now the adult child of an alcoholic. Throughout his youth, his father was chronically unemployed, drunk, and abusive. They often lived on the street or in vacated houses or buildings. His mother, whom he loved very much, was a passive woman who followed her husband from place to place and always did odd jobs trying to help pay for food and clothing. Life was very sad and painful. My patient described himself in his adult life as a one-time "hopeless alcoholic" who one day looked at his own life and just quit drinking.

Very few people can just decide on their own not to drink and make it work! Most require professional help and Alcoholics Anonymous to accomplish that goal. Alcoholism is a disease that kills. I don't quite understand this patient's ability to overcome this illness practically overnight. Some may call it a spontaneous cure. I believe that he is an exceptional patient who summoned his inner strengths to be able to achieve this miracle. Today he is a successful professional, but he suffers from manic depression, which periodically renders him penniless from poor decisions made during his manic state. After stabilization was accomplished through medication, I asked him to draw quickly his illness, and this is his rendering:

Notice how the peaks and valleys accurately represent the ups and downs of manic depression. He now sees himself as more stable due to therapy and experiences fewer extreme highs and lows. He also understands the power of negative thoughts and won't indulge in them.

I asked one of my patients who had cancer to draw her illness. The first time that I saw her she told me that she intended to be well by spring— and I happen to believe people who are able to make feisty comments like that! This is her drawing of the cancer:

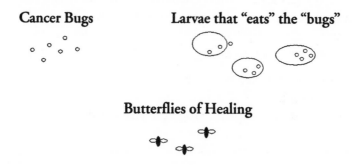

Cancer Bugs

Larvae that "eats" the "bugs"

Butterflies of Healing

If you guessed that she beat her cancer and used it as a source of strength, you are right! So many patients have told me that they have become thankful for their adversity because they have learned and gained so much from it. They appreciate life more fully and cherish friendships and family. They experience a change in their values and in what they perceive as really important. You can see it in their eyes.

Now it is your turn. Draw how you visualize your illness, whether it is depression, substance abuse, codependency, anxiety, or a bad relationship. You need to use only one color, and the drawing needs a form or a face or a scene—and give it a title.

Now let's examine what you have drawn. Answer these questions:

1. Are you in the drawing? Are there others there?
2. What are the sizes and proportions of the figures? How big are you?
3. What does the drawing represent?
4. Is it overwhelming or are you in control?
5. How do you feel while looking at it? How does the drawn figure feel?

Suppose your drawing seems bleak and overwhelming, and you find it frightening. Use your nondominant hand (in other words, if you are right-handed, use your left hand, or vice versa) to answer questions as you "talk" to your picture and listen to your soul. Ask yourself these questions:

1. What makes this picture scary?
2. How old am I?
3. How can I draw this picture to put me back in charge?

Draw your new picture (using your dominant hand). This time use bright colors; reduce the size of the scary part; make yourself larger. How do you feel now? More empowered? (Write it out.)

Okay, let's do one more picture. This time draw a picture of how you would like things to be. Again, do it in colors with streams of light. Is there fear?—or are you getting in touch with your soul? (Write it out.)

Write a verbal description of how your first picture differs from the second and third. Read your description (out loud, please!) and listen carefully.

Show your artwork to a close friend or family member and get that person's interpretations. You have now received a peek into your unconscious and have made a connection with your soul!

Let me teach you how to benefit from "dream work" . . .

Dr. Carl Gustav Jung[16] is the founder of analytical psychology and was a close colleague of Sigmund Freud early in the twentieth century. Jung was fascinated by another of humanity's symbols apart from art—dreams. He believed in something he called the *collective unconscious,* something through which we are all connected, which is defined as an inherited universal knowledge that continues to develop in an evolutionary fashion. The collective unconscious is a source of deep subconsciousness containing archetypes, representations of ancient spiritual wisdom and emotions. Jung would probably agree that this wisdom that we all possess originated with our creator.

To explain this common stream that unites us, Jung studied myths and symbols from many cultures. His work was significant because it joined the natural sciences (biology, chemistry, physics) with the humanities (art, history, languages, music). With our recently increased knowledge about the connections between psyche and soma, or mind and body, it is now apparent that his attempt to explain this connection was an early revolutionary idea. Jung used dreams to help interpret our archetypal messages and resolve psychological problems. Dreams are yet another way to peer into your unconscious and to become introspective.

Everybody dreams, and that is a scientific fact. The problem is that many people don't use this "messenger" because they have problems with recall, and often they just don't recognize the benefits that can be gleaned from this source of personal experience. Paying attention to dreams can make you more complete and can make sense out of irrational behaviors or beliefs. Dreams can also be prophetic, soothing, and sometimes downright funny! So here's how to start your dream work:

Capturing a Dream

1. Before going to sleep, firmly tell yourself that you are going to remember your dream.
2. Keep a pad and pencil next to your bed within easy reach.
3. As you awaken in the morning, don't get up until you have jotted down a few words about the main elements of the dream, any feelings, where you were, any symbols or images.
4. Later, go back and write in more detail what you can recall.
5. Be patient and persistent. This may take some practice.

Fritz Perls,[17] an advocate of Gestalt therapy, thought it important to "talk" to our dreams in order to encourage more dreams and to help with interpretation. He used two chairs—one for you and the second for the dream. As you look at the empty chair, which in actuality holds your dream, ask it a question such as "What are you trying to tell me?" Then, switch chairs and answer yourself as the dream! (I do recognize that this may sound silly, and indeed you may feel embarrassed, but try it—it works!)

The question-and-answer method is a good way to help interpret dreams, but sometimes the answer still seems nebulous. It is like not seeing the forest for the trees. You might want to ask someone who knows you well and whom you trust (or perhaps your doctor) for a little help. One book that I recommend is Anne Faraday's *The Dream Game*.[18]

About five years ago, I had a dream that changed my way of practicing psychotherapy and perhaps has a great deal to do with the writing of this book. In my dream my father and I were climbing a tall spiral staircase that led to a ladder. My dad, whom I love and trust, was behind me; and, given my fear of heights and a flimsy rope ladder, I felt nervous but safe since my dad was right there. At the top of the ladder a beautiful, deep-blue universe appeared with lovely silver stars. There were bands of purple and mauve colors and, as I floated around, I felt an enormous sense of peace—almost euphoria. It was as if my heavenly father were telling me to be more open, more spiritual, to reach more people, and to be aware of my fears but also to trust and climb higher. It's a message I want to share with you—*Trust and climb higher.*

Guardian angels . . .

When I was a young child, I attended St. Francis Elementary School. The nun who taught first grade was a loving teacher. Sister would have us sit on our little benches as we said morning prayers; however, we weren't allowed to sit exactly in the middle of our benches. Sister would always urge us to move over to the side a bit so that our guardian angel could sit down also. At age six that made a lot of sense to me because I certainly wouldn't have wanted my angel standing up all day. This sweet nun was the first to introduce me to my spiritual side. I have always been grateful for the security she nurtured in me through belief in my guardian angel.

The notion of the "child spirit" can be an important healing entity . . .

Admittedly, when the idea about an "inner child" first became popular, I had my reservations about it. It just seemed nonsensical, but after some consideration, it occurred to me that this was just another variation on Sigmund Freud's description of the self. I prefer to conceptualize it as a child spirit with whom we may communicate and who is more like an angel. Furthermore, just as my guardian angel gave me a sense of protection from all outside events, the child spirit has a similar mission to perform. As an adult, I *know* there are angels all around us.

The child spirit is clearly a part of each of us. If you have come from a dysfunctional family, your child spirit is also the keeper of unhappy and sad feelings. Your child spirit remembers all of the abuse and violence, abandonment and shameful events that took place in your childhood. These unresolved issues are the unfinished business that must be completed in order to heal. The child-spirit concept thus becomes another "therapy from the soul," another helpful tool.

Your child spirit is who you really are, not who you have become. It is a direct link to your past as well as to your present and future. Your child spirit is God's love in action and should be cherished. Embrace this innocence; celebrate the purity and the love.

With a little coaxing and doing a relaxation exercise, the child spirit can be heard. This aspect of your self is the child who was not nurtured or taken care of and who craves attention and affection.

You may be resisting the idea of a child spirit and that's okay, but let me try to explain your reticence . . .

What has protected you in life and been the foundation of your survival is denial, disassociation, and depression. Now here I come, asking you to lay down those defenses and become vulnerable again. The road to good mental and physical health requires remembering old pain, accepting what happened, and developing self-love and trust. Patients will sometimes tell me that they hate themselves, and my response is, "Hate what happened to you. Be incensed with the perpetrator, not with yourself." Separate the abuse you endured from the person you are. Reach out to yourself. Grieve the innocence that was taken from you. Replace it with love. Find an old picture of yourself when you were four or six or ten. That is who is hurting. Take a good look at that sweet child and carry it in your mind.

To reach your child spirit, get into a comfortable position—preferably on a nice, cozy sofa or an overstuffed chair. Curl up the way you see children do and allow yourself to relax. Close your eyes and see a fluffy white cloud float by. Hop onto it and enjoy the sensation as you sink into that cloud and feel so secure. Notice how heavy your toes and feet feel against this softness. Allow a warm, white light to comfort your toes and feet and move up into your legs. Feel how relaxed and secure you feel. Let the cloud rock you gently. That soft, white light is now moving from your legs into your back, and you are aware of how good that feels. You are feeling more and more secure, warm and cozy. Now that soft white light streams up into your neck and down your arms into your hands. You have a warm, tingly sensation. You feel that healing light go into your chest and head, and soon you are basking in it. As you feel safer and safer and more relaxed and comfortable, see a beautiful little girl [boy] who looks just like you playing in a safe place where you used to play. Talk to her [him], ask her [him] how old she [he] is. Notice what she [he] is wearing, what game she [he] is playing. Tell her [him] that you love her [him] and that you will be back tomorrow. Throw her [him] a kiss and watch her [him] wave back as you begin to move slowly into a more alert and conscious state.

Write a description of your child spirit and how you are feeling.

Each time you visit your child spirit, you can increase your self-love through loving her [him]. Sometimes it takes patience to connect with this concept, but what you will learn is incredibly important.

In your conversations always affirm your love for her [him], tell her [him] that you are here to take care of her [him] and that when she [he] cries out you will listen. Invite her [him] into your arms and hold and cuddle her [him].

Reparenting . . .

In the past, when you have felt your child spirit's pain, you always identified it or interpreted it as a need for help. You may have answered that cry for help by giving her [him] drugs, alcohol, or food, by taking care of others, by becoming involved in self-sabotaging behavior with peers, family, and friends. You became depressed or angry and experienced all of the pain contained in the lower self.

Higher Self	Spiritual Love Sixth Sense	Health
	——————	
Lower Self	Body, Personality Fear Guilt Shame	Cancer of the Self

You heard critical and shameful messages from the parent inside you (see diagram above) who told you that you were lazy and no good and worthless, so you turned to bad relationships that were destructive and painful. The people with whom you chose to be close were very much like the parents with whom you had the most difficulty. Most of us crave our parents' approval—unconditional love—but so few actually get it. So the task is to reparent ourselves.

It is very difficult to resolve past injuries without talking about them. But let your child spirit do the work. Your pain is connected to a parent or other adult figure; that's what this is all about.

Not long ago I treated a young woman who came to my office complaining of low self-esteem . . .

She had a happy marriage to a husband who was loving and supportive but who had a background that made it difficult for him to be openly affectionate. He was somewhat of a loner, but my patient was always understanding and never doubted his love and commitment. My patient was actually quite stable but always felt the pain of her relationship with her mother.

During my patient's childhood, her mother was cruelly critical of her, and, as a result, "Lynn" fought depression. Depression is described as "anger turned inward," but as we begin to unravel its origin, we have found it is associated with loss. In Lynn's case, she had felt abandoned by this emotionally remote, angry, and degrading mother. So as an adult, Lynn had picked up where her mother had left off. She minimized all of her accomplishments and set herself up for self-defeating behavior—thus, in a sense, proving "Mom" was right after all! Lynn did well at her job, but at the slightest hint of the possibility of a promotion, she would become paralyzed with fear and would play out her mother's "prophecy." She would suddenly be late with a project deadline or would even look for another job rather than risk taking a promotion. Lynn had insight into her problem, but just couldn't bring herself to embrace her potential because in effect she would be "betraying" her mother.

Lynn had been reared in her father's religion and took the Ten Commandments very seriously. "Honor thy father and mother" meant to Lynn agreeing with everything they said. When Lynn was an adolescent around age sixteen, the bottom fell out. Her father, whom she loved and admired, lost his job. Even though, financially, things were fine, he became very depressed. Once her haven, he began lecturing her several times a week about sex and men. This was always done when he used alcohol. Not only did her mother not rescue Lynn from these humiliating sermons, but she seemed to sanction them. When her father was sober, even though depressed, he was still capable of showing his love and support for Lynn, something she never received from her mother.

Lynn remained a loyal and loving daughter to both parents, and the idea of confronting her mother was unacceptable because of her religious beliefs. Yet she had to get it out. Lynn was blessed with a loving sister who helped her validate her feelings, much to her relief. But because her self-concept was still damaged, we did some child-spirit work. The following is her child spirit letter to her mother, which she wrote with her nondominant hand.

Dear Mom,

You have hurt me so very much. All I wanted was your love and approval. All I got was your rage and anger. You told me I was never going to amount to anything. You mocked my religious faith. You favored my brother and sister. I believed your judgments. You were cruel and mean and left me to take care of the house and little brother.

You were jealous of my relationship with Dad. When he became depressed, you didn't protect me from his lectures on sex. I felt so humiliated. I have been so hurt by you yet I feel guilty when I don't call you. You were not a good mother. I love you but I don't like you. I know you were sick and probably couldn't help it, so I do forgive you.

Lynn

And the following letter is written with the dominant hand, as if her mother were responding:

Dear Lynn,

I am so sorry that I did all of those things to you. You are a sweet, beautiful, intelligent person, and I should never have abused you as I did. It was my poor self-image that raged at you and that was wrong. You are a wonderful daughter, and I am sorry that I made you feel so bad.

It was wrong of me to make fun of your religious faith. I know now how that must have hurt you. I dumped my responsibilities on you and then tore you down instead of praising you. I took out on you the anger I felt toward your father. You are a sensitive, loving person and those lectures should not have occurred. I didn't protect you the way I should have. I have no excuses, but I want you to know how proud I am of your vast accomplishments and how very sorry I am for all of the undeserved pain that I caused you. Please forgive me.

I love you very much, my precious child.

Love, Mom

So, now it is your turn to do some healing . . .

Ask your child spirit to write a letter to your parent or parents:

1. Use your left hand if you are right handed, or vice versa.
2. Get in touch with your child spirit and let your child spirit compose the letter.
3. Describe the hurts or injustices; get it all out.
4. Thank your child spirit for his (her) bravery.

After reading your child spirit's letter, respond by writing a letter back that is supportive and loving—the way a healthy parent should talk to a small child.

1. Address each issue that your child spirit discussed.
2. Use your dominant hand.
3. Be the parent you wish you had had.

Kelly's story . . .

I treated a young woman in a group therapy session that I hold at the hospital. This lovely twenty-five-year-old was profoundly depressed, the unfortunate result of an abominable childhood. Her parents divorced when she was about three years old, and her father eventually went to prison for life. (He, by the way, is the supportive parent!) Kelly's mother went through several husbands, and Kelly was physically, emotionally, and sexually abused. Her mother was an alcoholic, who often left Kelly in charge of her younger brothers. After years of abuse, Kelly left home at age fourteen and went to live with her aunt. One night a fire swept through the home in which her brothers, mother, and stepfather lived. Her mother and stepfather escaped, but the boys died. Kelly blamed herself for their deaths because she felt that if she had not run away, she somehow could have saved them.

She loved her brothers dearly, and in despair from the intensity of her guilt and grief she turned to drugs and alcohol. Soon these did not provide the escape to peace she needed so desperately, so she tried suicide. Kelly is no quitter, however. She had the immense courage to turn her pain inside out, to try to make some sense out of her misery and the ordeals of her childhood.

By chance, Kelly came across an article and picture of "Mary Ellen"[19] who, in 1874, was the first child ever to have a documented child abuse case argued in court. So Kelly wrote her a letter. In Kelly's words, "I origi-nally wrote this letter to Mary Ellen, but found out later that I had written this letter to myself as well." Here is Kelly's child-spirit letter:

Letter to an Abused Child (1992)

Dearest Mary Ellen,

You do not know me, but I know you.

I want you to know that what has happened to you is *not* your fault.

You are a most precious child of God, undeserving of the barbaric treatment you have received at the hands of a very sick person.

I know it is hard for you to believe the things that people tell you — so many have lied to you — but please know that I will be there for you — I want to help you through all this pain you are suffering. I want to hold you in my arms and tell you and show you that I love you.

I want to hold you when you cry, and when you are angry and frightened.

I want to teach you to laugh and sing and play.

I want to wrap you up in love and take the hurt away.

I want to show you that you deserve a chance to live — so far you have only survived.

If you will let me I will take your hand and I will be there to protect you and guide you.

If you will let me love you, just a little, you can see that what you have been taught is not love — not even close.

It's not your fault — you do not deserve this kind of life.

I know this is scary for you. You don't know how to accept love and believe in it.

I want you to know that you have a right — God given — to be happy, to love and be loved, to grow and learn, and go to school, and have friends, and wear pretty clothes. You also have the right to say no to people when they are scaring you. You have the right to get angry and cry, you have the right to own yourself and be happy.

Take my hand, sweet, sweet child, let me help you through the dark to the light side of life.

Let me shower you with all the love and care you need and deserve.

Let me protect you and make you safe.

Let me love you, precious child.

All of my love to you,

Kelly

Kelly's battle is not over, but at least she is now out of the hospital, and she has made a commitment to live. She tells me that I am in her heart and prayers always, for which I am profoundly honored. She searches for meaning, but in her quiet dignity her courageous eloquence has taught me a great deal about the power of love and faith. At twenty-five years of age, Kelly's wisdom is greater than that learned in most lifetimes. She, too, is in my heart and prayers.

In an earlier session we discussed the importance of "reframing"—taking an event and changing the way we look at it . . .

Our example was Mary, who suffered from post-traumatic stress disorder. When she "rescripted and reframed" the event, she was able to turn feeling helpless and terrified into strength and survival.

Patients come into my office all of the time and describe their life or situation in terms of a metaphor. When we communicate a concept by linking it to something else, we create a metaphor. It is a shorthand method to explain how we feel. Some examples of metaphors are the following:

- I am between a rock and a hard place.
- I'm carrying the world on my shoulders.
- Well, I guess it's back to the old grindstone.
- Getting him to pick up his clothes is like pulling teeth.
- Life is like waiting for the other shoe to drop.
- Life is like bittersweet chocolate.
- My head feels like an explosion took place.
- Marriage is like the old ball and chain.

You have probably heard these metaphors all of your life—from parents, teachers, friends, and employers. If you are like most people, you found your metaphors by osmosis and used them to fit the situation. But these metaphors we borrow can be very toxic. They reinforce a sense of powerlessness and despair. They imply a lack of choice, and often the message is yet another negative—"Grin and bear it." They tend to generate helplessness and hopelessness.

1. So the first thing I would like you to do is list all of the metaphors you can remember:

2. Now, I would like you to fit them into categories and add more as you go along:

Relationships	Example:	My husband—the old hag.
		My kids—the rug rats.
Work	Example:	It's time to put my shoulder to the plow.
		A day late, a dollar short.
Life	Example:	The world is a cold place.
		You work hard all of your life and then you die.
		Life is like being in Tiffany's without money.

3. Now examine what you have written. What type of messages do the metaphors convey? Do they make you feel better or worse? Do you feel powerless or empowered?

4. This is the fun part. Change those toxic metaphors to create love, promise, and wonder. Write down each metaphor. Beside each, "reframe" it and give it optimism and joy. For example,

Old	**New**
Life is like bittersweet chocolate.	So add sugar!
Life is like being in Tiffany's without money.	Life is a motivator.
My husband—the old hag.	My loving partner in life.

5. Reexamine your new list and see how it can affect your outlook and future. Make a commitment to yourself to take advantage of these wonderfully hopeful and empowering thoughts. In Texas we have a modification on the old saying "If life serves you lemons, make lemonade!"; creative farmers have taken cow "paddies" (dried excrement) and made them into Frisbees and, by howdy, how they have sold!

Metaphors can help you see yourself differently . . .

It's time to create a "name metaphor" that describes you positively. Remember back when you were a child how some friends may have given you and themselves nicknames. I often work with adolescents who prefer to go by these "name metaphors," and I marvel at some of their choices. I have one patient who calls himself "Bear." This youngster lost a parent and is doing grief work. He is small for a sixteen year old and certainly does not appear threatening, but "Bear" has always felt empowered by his name and has conveyed that self-confidence to his peers. The name has also served as a source of inner strength in dealing with his loss. Another youngster I am treating calls herself "Slick." This adolescent was severely sexually and physically abused but survived the abuse and is dealing with it—because she is "slick" in getting out of bad situations!

Please be aware that none of these techniques works immediately, and none is a panacea. You have spent all the years of your life reaching this point, so learning a new process won't produce results overnight. If you are doing all of the exercises, however, and being introspective and using therapy from the soul, things will definitely improve.

Inner Guidance Meditation can produce amazing results . . .

What the ancients knew many civilizations ago, we are now recognizing and legitimating—the critical need for meditation. Whether you call it self-hypnosis, relaxation therapy, imagery, or meditation, the processes are similar and so are the results.

Dr. O. Carl and Stephanie Simonton[20] began using meditation—the relaxation of the body and mind along with guided imagery—giving specific direction to the unconscious in the treatment of terminally ill cancer patients. Their results were very amazing indeed, as outlined in their book *Getting Well Again.* They proved the power of the mind over the body. By getting to the subconscious, memories can emerge and messages can be heard.

I teach almost all of my patients to meditate because it helps with stress reduction and increases energy levels, but, what is most important, it allows them to connect to the "inner healer." I instruct my patients to get into a comfortable position and to lie down on my sofa. I make certain that the room is darkened and quiet and ask that they concentrate on the sound of my voice. When I do child-spirit work (see Session 10), I use the previously described method of induction.

I recommend daily meditation to start your day or to do during the afternoon. When you meditate, let your mind *see* specific scenes, places, things, and events. Imagine how things would look if you could have your wishes granted. Try to involve all of the senses. One of my favorite images — because I love the ocean—is to have someone take a trip to the beach and feel the warmth of the sun and *feel* the lovely breeze, *hear* the sea gulls calling, *smell* the ocean, *touch* the beautiful white sand, and *see* the gentle waves.

Meditation and prayer are very similar. It's a way to become in touch with our creator and to experience the gentle feelings of love and hope. It is an active part of grace. I like to talk to God—a lot—to recap what's going on and any problems that I am having. I talk about my children and my patients, and I try to be thankful for all that's good and happy in my life. It's surprising what you can learn by being quiet after one of those talks! In order to experience some of God's wisdom, you have to hold still. You complicate things when you are busy listening to your mind rather than to God! You may begin to wonder, "Who is saying what?" Talk to God with humility and openness; feel and hear his message.

Session 11 _____

Anger

_____

Issues we will discuss in Session 11:

- **Destructive anger** — As the result of painful childhoods, some people learn to turn anger against themselves and others externalize anger and violate those around them.
- **Physiological changes** — Effects of anger can be physical with symptoms that can actually be measured.
- **Biological rage** — Alzheimer's disease, Huntington's chorea, tumors, head injuries, birth injuries, convulsions are only some of the possible causes of rage suffered by some people.
- **Anger patterns** — Most of us fall within specific patterns of behavior in regard to the way we deal with or exhibit anger.
- **Self-anger** — Self-sabotaging behavior is often about being angry at yourself.
- **Appropriate confrontation** — Learn how to confront those who make you angry and turn anger into something constructive.
- **Empowerment** — Primal screaming, mattress work, breathing techniques.

Several years ago a man who was about thirty-eight years old came to see me about difficulties controlling his anger . . .

He was single, never married, but had had three or four long-term relationships. He grew up in the Midwest and was the eldest of four boys. His father worked in an agriculture-related field. My patient described his parents as "hard-working Germans from the old school."

Ed was a good student and was never in trouble, yet he lived a life of fear and pain, the result of his father's brutal beatings. His father belittled his sons, telling them they were worthless, selfish, lazy, and stupid. Mere eye contact with his father could be enough to provoke a beating. The boys were never allowed to cry, regardless of the pain. My patient could not recall his mother being there to protect them or intervene on their behalf, but he viewed her as loving and a good mother. Additionally, two of the brothers were "slow learners." Apart from the beatings and berating, the father would also throw them around the room and bang their heads against the wall. Perhaps this explains why they were "slow learners."

My patient was soft spoken, well mannered, but much to the alarm of his coworkers, Ed would punch himself and call himself names if he became angry. Sometimes this self-abuse would result in black eyes. Ed continued the lifelong pattern where his father had left off.

Over the years I have treated many patients who were dealing with issues of anger. Some, like Ed, turned their violence toward themselves; some externalized their anger and violated others, while some internalized their anger and became depressed or suffered physically with heart disease, cancer, hypertension, and the like.

Anger is a basic emotion, but one that we don't like to discuss. Yet this very lack of discussion generates and escalates more anger. Anger is a learned response, usually from our parents. The purpose of anger is to neutralize, protect, or avoid anxiety, which rears its ugly head whenever we feel an interpersonal threat. When a child is frustrated, usually the result of challenging the authority of mom or dad, he or she notices this amazing range of anger that is generated by the parent. So the child then makes the intuitive connection between the uncomfortable and powerless anxiety feelings that he or she has used to try to manipulate parents through tears and the extreme power gained by converting those feelings into anger! Anger is distinctly more powerful than anxiety. The degree and method to which a child uses this "power" can be helpful or hurtful, and the stakes increase as he or she becomes an adult.

The price some people pay for anger is feeling victimized by forces beyond their control, such as might occur in employee/employer problems, finances, and relationships. They feel that advantages and luck are for *other* people and that they themselves are powerless and weak. Often they are not even aware of these feelings, especially if they come from a family where anger and conflict were not allowed or discussed. Even if they do temporarily overcome their feelings of intimidation and speak up, they are consumed with guilt for having done so and then give up on life. For others, they fear that if they let out their anger, they might hurt someone or that if they really let out their anger fully, they could go crazy. The real truth is that unexpressed anger can lead to depression, suicide, a major illness, or a violent outburst of rage—the very same outcomes people are attempting to avoid by bottling up their anger.

I work with many dysfunctional families, and if I had to name one of the most toxic emotions with which they deal, it would be anger . . .

Anger is an emotion that generates physiological changes and produces feelings that often impact on your self-image and perception of life events. Anger can serve several behavioral functions. For example, anger may announce to others by various means of expression how you are feeling or what your position on a specific issue may be. It may be a warning that signals an action. Anger can be an effective but damaging way to control or influence others. Anger is a necessary emotion that helps us to survive in a sometimes difficult life. It is an emotion, and, like any other emotion, it is OK to feel it. Anger can help us find the strength necessary to stop feeling helpless and to feel empowered rather than victimized. It most assuredly does not have to culminate in violence.

Anger produces a wide range of physiological changes—many of which can actually be measured by chemical assays, EEGs, blood tests, and computers. Some typical responses include

> changes of muscle tension
> vascular changes, flushing or paling
> sweating
> clenching of fists or teeth
> dry mouth
> difficulty thinking
> change in voice
> fright
> aggression.

One very provocative finding by researchers investigating anger was that although some people felt physically ill by anger, others reported a feeling of exhilaration. This tends to lend credibility to those of us who see anger, when appropriately channeled, as a great motivator. People tend to be motivated either away (avoidance) from pain or toward (approach) pleasure. The approachers may find their situation so terrible and become so angry that they will use that anger as fuel to accomplish greatness. There are countless examples, like William Henley who wrote *Invictus,* which you read a few sessions back. Some common comments you may hear are, "Well, I'll show you," "I am going to make them eat those words," or "I don't care what Dad said, I will be successful."

Researchers have also tried to identify and categorize things that make people angry. One category was "stupid inanimate objects"—things that don't work, like a pen out of ink, vending machines that take your money, and so forth. A second category was "special aversions" such as little habits or quirks people have that are annoying—for example, men who actually believe that wearing a medallion around their neck is attractive or sexy! But the third category, "injustice to others," was the one most people identified as the most anger arousing. Insults, cheating, abuse, and being condescending were high on the list.

Many researchers have looked at biological conditions . . .

Some people, for seemingly no reason at all, can erupt spontaneously into a rage, creating verbal and physical violence. A tumultuous storm in the brain produces just such expressed rage and has now been identified as a seizure.

Allergies, especially to certain foods, have reportedly produced rage, though this is very rare. Disease or damage associated with the temporal lobe in the brain, Alzheimer's disease, Huntington's chorea, tumors, and head injuries are causes that produce attacks of rage. Further, genetic and other organic defects, birth injuries, and infantile convulsions are frequently reported as possible causes for the rage suffered by some people.

Dorothy O. Lewis studied juvenile delinquents imprisoned for violence and found that physical trauma corresponds directly to increasingly violent behavior. Again, angry, abusive parents not only "show" children how to act and respond, but in the course of the abuse, they may also inflict neurological injuries that cause violence. It must be stated here, however, that only about one-third of physically- or sexually-abused people continue the same pattern with their children. Most, through education and personal strength, have learned more appropriate methods to deal with anger and go out of their way to stop the cycle. You may remember my telling you about "Billy," whose neurological deficit and outbursts of rage were directly related to his horrid physical abuse. Billy was a tragic example of the impact of rage.

Anger then tends to be associated with incidents of which you are aware (for example, you see someone flip you off while you are driving) and with ones of which you are not aware (for example, something triggers a suppressed feeling, or, less often, there is a biological problem). It is also associated with how we perceive an incident—our own interpretation of an event. In a nutshell, anger can be either self-generated or a reaction to environmental demands, and the sources can be physiological, emotional, cognitive, or behavioral. While you cannot control *feeling* angry, you can control how you act upon it.

Most of us fall within specific patterns in expressing anger that coincide with our personalities . . .

Now that we have defined anger, considered its purpose, identified bodily changes, looked at some "causes" of anger as well as some of the common triggers that evoke the anger response, we need to focus on anger patterns. Remember that you may not have just one pattern; sometimes they overlap.

In Session 7 we touched on personality types as they relate to dealing with stress. This time we will use the four types—sanguines, cholerics, phlegmatics, and melancholics—as they relate to anger. I have theorized that the way in which we manage anger is directly correlated to our personalities which directly correlates to our perceptions.

The happy-go-lucky **sanguines**, who can never get anything organized, become less competent when dealing with anger. They tend to let others "take over," and this increases their personal rage. Sanguines are likely to develop physical or emotional symptoms when anger is present in either the family or the work place. Anger is absolutely counter to their personality and self-concept, so they minimize or deny angry feelings. Some of their maladaptive techniques include masking their feelings with humor, avoidance, and development of psychosomatic complaints. They may react to these feelings by seeking greater togetherness in a relationship and can feel rejected easily if someone close to them wants more space or wants to end the relationship. Sanguines may act out their anger by impulsive and destructive acts.

Cholerics have very definite ideas about anger management and absolutely know what's best for themselves and others. They move in quickly to advise, rescue, and take over when anger is in the air. They tend to respond to anger swiftly with great emotional intensity and fighting. They have a short fuse and view others as the sole obstacle to making changes. They tend to project their own feelings and actions onto others and engage in repetitive cycles of "blowing up," which relieves tension but perpetuates old patterns. They rarely see themselves at fault and will expend high levels of energy trying to change others' behavior. Assuming personal responsibility is not their style, and often their anger leads to attacks of rage, verbal assaults, and sometimes violence. In their eyes it is justified because they are never wrong.

Melancholics deal with anger by looking for a place to hide and by seeking emotional distance. In fact, in order to avoid anger, they may discontinue a significant relationship rather than sit down and work things out. They turn their anger inward and often are depressed as a result. Melancholics feel ill equipped to deal with conflict, and confrontation is out of the question for them. Because of their introversion, they fear losing control should they ever express anger. They are often extremely critical of their partners, but their criticism is a projection of their own feelings of insecurity and inadequacy.

Phlegmatics are usually the products of parents who taught them that nice people do not get angry. As a result, they avoid conflict and people who do get angry. They believe that people should try to hold anger in, even when they feel a situation is unjust. They do not like upsetting the status quo. Consequently, they suffer from gastrointestinal disorders, hurt feelings, and depression. Because they tend to be indifferent and indecisive, any kind of conflict resolution is all the more problematic.

As I mentioned before, these personality styles can overlap, so you may discover that your anger pattern is mixed. The important insight you have just developed will determine more helpful and less destructive ways to manage your anger. Of equal importance is the information you may have gleaned about your spouse's patterns.

When we spoke earlier in Session 2 about Maslow's Need Theory, we really identified the core issue in anger. Every baby born in this world craves love and attention—the emotional attachment on which good mental health is predicated. When a baby looks into his mother's eyes and experiences her love and approval, self-love emerges. When this primary basic need is not met, we experience rejection, and because of this pain, we develop fear. Thus we begin to defend ourselves, and this makes us angry. So here we have it, simply put:

unmet basic love =
　　　rejection =
　　　　　pain =
　　　　　　　fear =
　　　　　　　　　defense =
　　　　　　　　　　　anger.

And this is what anger is all about — lack of love.

We know from research and statistics that the majority of violent acts are committed in the home . . .

Our homes are supposed to be our sanctuaries, not our battle grounds. Yet the place where the need is greatest to give and receive love is also the place that makes us most vulnerable to pain and rejection. When things do not work out within an intimate relationship, the intensity of resulting anger is equal to the intensity of the original love. If you come from a home in which battering was modeled, you may repeat the pattern. If you come from a home where love was conditional and there was verbal battering, you may seek a mate who not only verbally batters, but may physically batter also. We do what we know. And so, in a desperate attempt to get the "love" experienced by the abuse, emotionally or physically battered spouses return to their abusers. Their unconscious reason for returning is to make right the family-of-origin relationship and at last be loved. It is very easy to sit in judgment over this kind of irrational behavior, but the subconscious motivation is more complex than it appears on the surface.

Domestic violence is unacceptable and wrong. If you are in this type of relationship, you must seek immediate help through a battered women's shelter or from your local police. They can steer you to the appropriate professional help.

Keep an anger diary . . .

So now it is time to become more analytical and keep a diary of your anger. For the next few weeks, write about your incidents of anger and answer the following four questions:

1. What is going on that makes me angry?

2. What is the core issue here for me?

3. What are my responsibilities?

4. How can I change this situation and achieve parity and peace?

Notice that there is no question about blame or guilt, just responsibility.

Self-anger . . .

You have become the product of a vicious cycle that began with learned low self-esteem, inadequate self-love, and progressed to fear and dependency; this ultimately results in self-disgust and self-anger. You may have become angry at yourself for

> not taking care of yourself physically
> overeating, undereating, drug, alcohol, and other addictions
> saying "yes" when you mean "no"
> not listening to yourself, but doing what others tell you to do
> being forgetful
> feeling like a giant screw-up
> being hopeless and helpless.

Does it sound familiar? This is anger at a superficial level. But after working through the discovery sessions, you should know now why you do it and begin to stop persecuting yourself. Being responsible and taking action against self-anger is the next step. God gave us the emotion of anger to use constructively, and self-anger is not constructive. The road back means recognizing that you are getting angry at the wrong person! You need to identify the anger with the appropriate individual, such as an abusive spouse or parent, an unreasonable boss, a friend who betrays you—not "just" anger. But since you are afraid to confront these folks because you fear their anger or withdrawal of love, you instead create additional and unjust self-anger. You can't live this way. Anger that is just is a defense against being taken advantage of or abused. The test of justness is asking yourself the simple question *Is my anger the result of someone intentionally hurting me?*

How we become angry is based on the individual's personal appraisal of the situation, and that appraisal method originated from the individual's past experiences. For example, an offhand, kidding remark might make one person chuckle, but another person may experience devastation. The first person's appraisal or interpretation might be harmless humor; the other person may see it as humiliating and demeaning! If you were cruelly teased and treated abusively as a child, you may play those old tapes and hear toxic voices emerging. Obviously, our appraisals are not always rational, but this little technique works:

1. Write down an anger incident.

2. Write down your appraisal.

3. Look at the feelings that were generated and write down where they came from in your past.

4. Write an alternate appraisal.

This is a form of sensitivity training—helping you to become more aware of why things make you angry. The more often you employ this method, the less angry you will become.

When anger is just, it needs to be addressed. Not expressing it leads to resentment, hostility, and escalating anger. We all have experienced people who seem angry all of the time, yet try to disguise and hide their anger. These people have never learned appropriate confrontation and spend their lives giving subtle digs, being slow and making people wait, and demonstrating other passive-aggressive behaviors.

My idea of confrontation is not a bloody battle that generates intense heat. I view it as a defuser, to prevent outbursts, to clarify a misunderstanding, to exchange helpful information that will increase intimacy and good feelings. The elements of an appropriate confrontation follow.

Appropriate Confrontation

1. Carefully consider what is involved in the matter before you turn it into open conflict.

2. Confront the right person in a private place at a convenient time and

limit the conflict to the here and now. Do not bring up old issues for ammunition.

3. Discuss only one issue at a time and use the "hard on the issue, soft on the person" approach. Planning and organization of thoughts should be used prior to the confrontation.

4. Use "I" statements and supportive communication (see Session 8). "You" messages are a statement of condemnation; using "I" conveys a feeling.

5. Avoid global generalizations such as "always," "never," "everybody," "all of the time."

6. Confront the behavior, not the attitudes. Do not launch a general attack on the other's personality—no character attacks.

7. No mind reading; no counterattacks. Accept the other's statement as his or her perception. No hitting below the belt.

8. Take responsibility for *your* actions and feelings. Try to analyze your own participation in the problem, not the other party's participation.

9. Understand that your perception could be wrong.

10. State the problem in behavioral terms, such as "When _____ happens, I feel _____ because _____."

11. Use "active listening" technique.

12. Make sure that your emotions are proportionate to the crime.

13. Be emotionally supportive. Do not be concerned with winning or losing. What is important is that the problem is solved.

14. Make a plan to make certain all of these rules are followed.

Now let's explore what you've learned so far . . .

1. Describe one example of a confrontation you handled recently.

2. How did you feel about it?

3. How many elements of an appropriate confrontation did you employ?

4. What do you think you need to change or add to be more effective?

Remember this takes practice! Perhaps you may have said in your answer to question number 4 that you need to learn how to deal with the other person's anger. Being the recipient of a barrage of anger—a frontal attack directed at you— is uncomfortable at best, especially given your fears of rejection, abandonment, or withdrawal of love. Being assertive and standing your ground is important, especially if you have been controlled or manipulated to acquiesce by another's anger.

To reduce the anger level, try to listen to your partner while maintaining eye contact. Avoid taking the anger personally—it may be that your partner is just ventilating. Suggesting that your partner "relax" or "calm down" tends to escalate and intensify the anger. There is little benefit in trying to "reason" or "argue" with someone who is raging. While you cannot control another's behavior, you can control yours. Gently state in a low, soft voice that you need a time out, but that you would be willing to listen in about fifteen minutes. Getting a glass of water may help to break up the cycle. Sometimes, suggesting that you both move to a different room is useful. If, in spite of these suggestions, the anger continues to escalate, take care of yourself, which may mean leaving. No one should *ever* tolerate abuse.

You can gauge fairly accurately the level of anger by the words used. At low levels people use words like "I feel irritated or annoyed." At medium levels words such as "mad," "angry," or "upset" are used. At high anger levels the words change to "irate," "furious," and "enraged." The voice volume increases at each level. I tell patients that recovery from anger has to precede the medium level and definitely the high level. Try to nip things in the bud by awareness of the intensity and by dealing with issues as they arise. Expressing a sincere desire to help as soon as you recognize that your partner is angry as well as avoiding blame tends to prevent escalation.

Sharing the information you have received about anger control with your partner can be very beneficial. Obviously, you would want to select a time when things are peaceful and your partner would be the most receptive.

Empowerment

Primal Screaming

One of the best methods that I suggest to my patients to release anger is primal screaming. I encourage them to turn up the radio so as to not distress the neighbors and go into their closet with a big pillow to scream into. I have them close the door, with the lights on or off, and just scream. You may be a bit hesitant, so start out slowly and build. Keep doing it until you can scream no more. To get started, it may be helpful to think of an event or person that upset you and just yell and scream as loudly and from the gut as much as you can. If you do it correctly, you should feel a sense of relief. The more often that you use this technique, the more effective it will become.

Breathing

Breathing exercises are a wonderful preventative method to avoid angry outbursts. When you do them, your body should be relaxed, and you should concentrate on your exhale. First, stand upright with your feet slightly apart. Breathe in through your nose to the count of four until your lungs are fully expanded. Next, rapidly exhale the air through your mouth and make a loud whoosh sound as you do it; at the same time drop your upper torso to the floor, bending your knees. Finally, when you are very relaxed, slowly get up, inhaling to a count of eight. Once you are standing erect, exhale again and repeat the exercise.

Total Body Relaxation

This exercise is a highly relaxing experience that you should do daily. First, lie down on the floor, close your eyes, and go through your body progressively tensing up and letting go. Begin with your feet and stretch and release each body part from toe to head. You should allow twenty minutes for this technique and concentrate on feeling relaxed, heavy, and peaceful. Try doing it at the same time daily.

Punching Bags

One item I frequently recommend for adults with anger issues, as well as for adolescents, is a punching bag. With gloves on hands, picture an anger issue and let the bag have it. One can do preventive work as well, so I encourage patients not to wait until they become angry; rather, box the bag daily just to blow off steam.

Mat or Mattress Work

First, get an old mattress or mat and lay it on the floor. Next, kneel at one end of the mattress with a large pillow in front of you. Hold your hands in a fist over your head and come down as hard as possible on the pillow. Repeat this several times. Now, it is time to throw what we call in Texas a "wild-eyed hissy fit"—otherwise known as a tantrum. Just like a two-year old, lie down flat on the mat, kicking your feet and pounding your fists, loudly screaming, "I am angry!" and then scream what you are angry about. Go until you can't go any more. Repeat the exercise as often as necessary until the anger dissipates and you feel empowered.

Final Thoughts . . .

We come into this world with God's love. He looks upon us even now with all of our imperfections as a perfect reflection of his likeness. And his love is unconditional. Anger is something that we have learned, and the price we have paid for that lesson is the distance we put between ourselves and God's love. Yes, some people have been deeply wounded, and their scars are direct proof of the injustice and agony they have suffered. The tragedy is that they allow their anger to immobilize their growth and the promise of love. We sometimes get so caught up in being right that we forget about being happy.

It is essential to do our anger work, but it is also essential to let go. No one can change what has happened, or change the people who trespassed against us. It would be foolish to deny our anger and pain, but we can ask the Holy Spirit for help. Say aloud:

I am angry, but I am willing to let it go. Help me to see my situation differently.

Lean on the Holy Spirit and let it do the impossible. You have suffered enough and deserve the love for which you have longed. It is time to move toward God.

Session 12 _____

Forgiveness

_____

Issues we will discuss in Session 12:

- **Being unforgiving** — When we are unable to forgive, the costs are too high in personal failures.
- **Faith** — The foundation of our very existence and our ability to forgive is faith, which is a belief in God or a higher power.
- **Charity** — Only when we express and extend our hearts may we feel forgiven.
- **Grace** — Forgiveness is helped by grace, which represents God's total unconditional love for us.
- **Self-forgiveness** — Being able to forgive others is impossible without being able to forgive yourself first.
- **Forgiving others** — Perpetually carrying around terrible memories is heavy baggage that impedes the process of forgiveness.
- **Heal yourself** — Steps to self-forgiveness enable you to replace old painful memories with fresh positive ones.

You have come a very long way, but now I must tell you that your real journey is just beginning. Linking your past to the present has been very enlightening for you, and, facilitated by your patience, the discovery process has answered, I hope, many of your questions—even those that hadn't occurred to you to ask. As you moved through the Sessions on healing and learned what you can do about your pain, the resulting insights have served as a prelude to a richer and healthier life for you. But the essential ingredient to a new beginning for a whole and fulfilled you is the ultimate challenge—forgiveness of others and of yourself, *all* of whom, including yourself, have done harm to you.

Forgiveness is not always easy. . .

Forgiving means that we must stop embracing our pain and turn away from destructive patterns, patterns that in a very sick and contradictory way have been our comforter as well as our tormentor. Immersed in our familiar pain, we always knew what to expect; we believed, in a distorted fashion, and we felt safe; we understood the "laws" of those patterns; and we clung to the darkness of those feelings as a child clings to his mother. But the price is too high. Being unforgiving costs us relationships because we cannot trust. It blinds us to being able to see our failures as growth experiences and opportunities. It costs us shame, guilt, and self-sabotage because we are convinced our self-hatred and loathing are truly deserved. And we have paid such a terrible price—mental anguish, anger, resentment, jealousy, and physical illness.

Enough!

Before we move into discussing some practical rules for learning how to forgive, I think it is important to look at the components of forgiveness: faith, charity, and grace.

Faith

Faith means the confidence, trust, and steadfast belief in a person or thing. For most of us that means believing in a higher power, intuition, God, or perhaps some a priori knowledge from eons ago. This belief is a deeply personal commitment often despite the apparent absence of proof of that person's or thing's existence. In its most primitive form, faith is the basis on which a small child stays with its mother, believing in her nurturing and protection. Even when a mother or father betrays that fundamental belief, "child-like faith" fuels the hope that this will change. One has only to look into the eyes of a hopeful orphan or foster child to see faith's presence. Faith is not something one teaches you, although certainly churches, temples, mosques, and other holy places of worship can foster this state of unshakable devotion. If faith is not a learned behavior, is it somehow part of our genetic coding, some tiny chromosome perhaps, or is it breathed into us at birth, allowing us to know that ultimately we all come from a loving teacher?

I have witnessed the power of faith bring forth a miraculous change in someone or in a situation, but I have also seen faith shattered when someone concedes the battle. At that moment the destruction of faith is expressed in despair, profound depression, and psychosis. Faith is the foundation for our very existence and our ability to forgive. It is a divine energy upon which we build our character and life. It is this very divinity that gives us the ability to ask "Who am I?" "Why am I here?"

These questions, asked even by the most desperate among us, imply the presence of our faith. Faith can be a beseeching of God or just a quiet feeling. In the final analysis faith provides us peace.

When I was a young mother, questioning my belief in Catholic doctrine, I wrestled with the idea of the necessity for formal religious education for my children. (By formal, I mean being taught "by the book" and usually by the nuns.) I tried to understand the need for celibacy (which meant priests and nuns could not marry), the alleged wickedness of practicing birth control unless it was the rhythm method, why women were treated as second-class humans, and why I felt that every time I had a thought or turned around I had committed a sin. These rules were not about God; they were about rules made in the sixth century.

My parents lived in Bethlehem, Connecticut, and in this town there is a convent called Regina Laudis. It was a cloistered convent, which meant that the nuns had little to do with life outside the protection of the monastic walls. I went to visit Mother Delores, who prior to becoming a nun had been a movie star (Delores Hart). She understood the secular and the nonsecular. I expressed my concerns as she listened sympathetically. She told me not to worry with formality, but to teach my children the awe of God, drawing from nature to provide examples such as the magnificence of the ocean or the delicacy of a flower. I have tried to do just that, instill in them that awe of God and increase their faith so that they may be capable of experiencing their creator's love.

When we have little faith or feel that self-forgiveness is elusive, the ability to forgive oneself and others is lost. Only when we come to embrace our creator do we become able to forgive and be forgiven.

Charity

Charity, another integral part of forgiveness, is the act of giving someone something out of benevolence with no expectation of any reward, material or otherwise. The gift does not always have to be material goods, but can be as simple and yet as dramatic as a soothing word and empathic listening. We usually think of charity in terms of giving something to the less fortunate, yet the opportunity for charity is all around us. People often fail to recognize that when they give a warm smile or do a simple considerate act, they are being charitable. Partially then, forgiveness is an act of charity. When you forgive another, you are acting in a charitable fashion, not just to that person but to yourself as well. Forgiveness is like charity in that you don't expect anything in return such as a change in the person who receives your gift, a reciprocal forgiveness, appreciation, or gratitude. There are no strings attached.

Extending one's self and one's love is a particular challenge when you believe that someone has severely harmed you and that they don't care. Now your gift is even greater! Giving a basket of fruit is easy when our pockets are full but becomes a challenge when they are not. So it is with forgiveness. Forgiving is easy when our self-image is high, and we feel like a loved child of God, but a challenge when our emotional pockets are shallow and empty.

Charity is necessary, however, because only when we express and extend our hearts may we feel forgiven. When patients complain to me that they feel empty, depleted, or angry, I often suggest to them that they do something nice for another—visit a nursing home or help cook a meal at a homeless shelter, for example. Diverting focus from yourself and looking after someone else's needs for a change is the best way I know to help yourself. In a fashion, doing for others is a little selfish because the serene yet exhilarating feeling that you get when you give is indescribable. Charity is God's messenger to others—a whisper from God that reminds us to love.

Grace

And so if faith is our foundation from God and charity is God's messenger, then grace is the protection of God's love. This is the third element of forgiveness. Grace is a manifestation of God's mercy and does not need to be earned—it just *is*.

In God's grace we grow, and to the extent that we allow grace in our lives, we expand our spirituality. Through grace our spiritual growth becomes our commitment to our creator, a commitment we accept as best we can. Because of our imperfection, we put limits on ourselves and often lose sight of our spirituality. It is grace that facilitates our forgiveness. Grace is the act of experiencing mercy and makes us realize that we are in God's favor and are beloved by him. Grace is total unconditional love.

Marianne Williamson contends that suffering is not a precondition of receiving grace, nor does the amount of suffering make one more worthy—that suffering is an overglorified state. How often we forget this. I don't think grace or God is about suffering and pain. In fact, I think God weeps when we are ill or feel lost. I think God is about love and forgiveness, and no matter what the circumstance, we are always in a state of grace when we allow God's love into our lives. We allow his love when we recognize that because we are all his children, we treat each other with respect and kindness. We allow his love when we do his work—looking for our meaning and purpose and performing those simplest of charities. We allow his love when we acknowledge his blessings—feeling your pain but feeling your goodness also. And we allow his love when we teach our children that unkindness is wrong and love is right.

All acts of forgiveness are inspired by grace.

Forgiveness of self . . .

Because you nurture from your own overflow, forgiving others is impossible without first forgiving yourself. Often patients have come to my office in great pain because their self-defeating behaviors have left them "just short" of maintaining a relationship, progressing in a career, finding happiness, and achieving success. They tell me things such as "I blew it," "I missed my golden opportunity." These patients clearly lack self-love and self-forgiveness. Long ago as a child when they were open and trusting, someone came along and said or did something that hurt them deeply, so they believed that person and built a wall to protect themselves. Someone taught them that they were less than perfect and that only perfection is what is acceptable. They came away feeling undeserving and, as Freud would express it, "stuck." Because of this judgment on their part about being "less than," when something wonderful comes their way, they make sure that they sabotage it. They can't believe that they are deserving. Even though God's grace is always there, they don't believe it, which renders them feeling helpless and hopeless. They don't know self-love or forgiveness.

Changing your mind about yourself is the first step toward self-forgiveness. We are indeed children of God, so is it not arrogant on our part to judge harshly his creation? All of us have made mistakes in our past, but we cannot allow those mistakes to define us. You may think of many mistakes that you have committed, but those mistakes are not who you are or who you can be.

There is an expression that says, "As you believe, so you are." It means that we always act consistently with our self-image. If you label yourself as unworthy, selfish, unkind, you will act in accord with that view. When those thoughts creep in, reminding yourself that you are a child of God may bring about the first step toward self-forgiveness. Allow yourself to be embraced by the Holy Spirit and ask that those unhealthy thoughts be cleansed into thoughts about healing.

Our Creator endowed us with free will. I certainly have not always made correct choices, so I say to myself, "OK, Ann, you have just messed up royally—so what are you going to do next?" That "next" has been a long time in coming. There was a time when that "next" often meant making an even bigger mess! And, of course, that was the springboard to guilt, anger, beating up on myself, and, did I mention, more guilt. I forgot that I was our Creator's child. I forgot about grace.

Now "next" means How can I turn this around? To whom must I make amends? (And that "whom" also includes me.) How can I repair the damage and turn this into a positive outcome? What is the lesson to be learned? Reconciliation is a humbling experience indeed, but from reconciliation our Creator's love is showered upon us and on the person to whom we are asking forgiveness.

Some people feel so far away from their Creator that they are unable to begin the process of feeling grace. For these people I suggest just being still, clearing their minds of as many distractions as they can, and being quiet and reverent. I ask them to concentrate on their breathing as they go deeper into a state of stillness. I caution them not to expect to hear a great voice or earth-shaking pronouncements, but with practice they will begin hearing some soothing messages. I encourage them to speak to God, which eventually leads to a state of grace.

I ask them to let go of their grip on pain and suffering in order to make room for their forgiveness. Our misery and pain are not a reflection of God's judgment, but rather are reflections of our own judgments. No one is as capable of punishing us as we are ourselves. Our ego is doing its best at all times to further the separation between God and his children. But you don't have to listen; you know now that you have a choice.

Forgiving others . . .

In Alcoholic's Anonymous there is an expression that says, "Let go and let God." Forgiveness is letting go—letting go of painful acts perpetrated against you, injuries caused by the negligence or ignorance of others, or vicious violations on your character. All forgiveness starts with our parents because they were our primary caretakers and role models. They showed us how adult men and women should act, and they were the original source for our self-images. Obviously, some did a better job than others. But whatever was done or not done, your peace and spiritual growth hinges on forgiving them. Christ said, "Father, forgive them for they know not what they do," and this is a good thought with which to start.

Few parents intentionally try by their actions to condemn their children to a life of misery. In their anger and ignorance they may have damaged us, but by looking at that anger we have learned that it serves a purpose—we are given the opportunity to choose otherwise. Our "faults" are our wounds—be they wounds inflicted by our mother or wounds inflicted by our father. By consciously acknowledging this, we can ask God's help in the forgiveness process. We can decide either to champion love or to succumb to fear, live with our furies or forgive and love them. Isolating specific memories and focusing on love helps us to "let go and let God."

Forgiving is like tossing a pebble into the water. Initially, there is a small circle, but soon the circle expands and gives rise to concentric circles, each originally spawned from that tiny little pebble. When you forgive, your act will be like that tiny pebble, one kindness becoming more and more encompassing with each person it touches.

Some people may say, "But I can't forgive what they have done. They were horrible and don't deserve my forgiveness." *They* may not, but *you* do. Perpetually carrying around terrible memories is extremely heavy baggage, a weight that keeps you mired in misery. Let go!

Acting as your own healer can be a new strategy for you . . .

Examining your conscience may be a bit like navigating through a mine field. The demons that reside there explode with pain at the slightest approach. This is an example of your old behavior patterns, which caused you to wallow in the shame, fear, and darkness; these patterns were self-flagellating and demeaning to your being. You need now to adopt a new strategy, one that does not guard your agony, but rather one that releases that pain through forgiveness. It's important to understand that by acting as your own healer you must embrace those painful incidences knowing that they originally helped to create the person you are. Reflect quickly on a strength or a kindness that you have done and replace that old painful memory with a fresh, new, loving one. Concentrate on how you want to live your life from now on and act upon it. Reliving your past shackles you to shame and helps no one. It zaps your strength and impedes your creativity. See yourself as whole and pure because as you believe, so will you be.

Step I to Self-Forgiveness

Faith   1. Talk to God or your higher power.

2. Identify an old shame, fear, or darkness.

Charity   3. Quickly reflect on a strength or kindness.

Grace   4. Visualize and concentrate on how you want to be and take action by seeing the new thought.

Once you identify an incident, do not allow yourself to dwell on it; immediately look at a positive characteristic, trait, or kindness. The next step involves reconciliation, the act of atoning for your wrongdoing. If what you want to forgive involved hurting someone else, go to that person and ask for their forgiveness. There are times when the injured party may not accept your apology, but that's OK. At least you have tried to make amends. If you fear reconciliation, just remember that your human dignity arises from God, who says "Be not afraid, for I am with you."

Step II to Self-Forgiveness

Faith   1. Examine whether your act hurt someone else.

Charity   2. Go to that person and ask for forgiveness. (This can be a humbling experience.)

Grace   3. If they cannot forgive you, understand that you have done your best, and now all you can do is pray for that person.

Be patient and gentle with yourself. Forgiveness takes time and patience and demands replacing old wrong-thinking behaviors with new ways of doing things. You will have to give up the comfort of those old patterns, which is a relatively small price for peace.

Forgiving others requires enacting faith, charity, and grace . . .

How strange that it is easier to forgive others who have harmed you rather than forgive *you* who have harmed you. But so it is.

Years go, and even today in some stores or companies, the owners would give out "green stamps" for spending a certain amount of money or coming up with cost- or time-saving ideas. You would then collect these stamps, which could be redeemed for free merchandise at a later date. Often, when I do conjoint or couple counseling, I will talk about the collection of "brown stamps" (old wounds or anger) that people put in a bag and drag around with them. At the slightest provocation or fight the individuals "spend" their brown stamps as ammunition against their mate. This ammunition sounds like this: "And I remember when your mother criticized me and you took her side!" or "You have been spending all our money from day one—remember on our honeymoon?!" or "You have *never* helped around the house." They drag out brown stamps even when that response has nothing to do with the controversy at hand. One can easily see that over the course of a relationship that bag could become very cumbersome. When it is appropriate during the course of counseling, I will then discuss the idea of forgiving—which means throwing away those brown stamps permanently and enacting faith, charity, and grace.

Faith takes strength. If you are really motivated to lay down your burdens and change your attitude, forgiveness is the correct path. The steps to forgiving someone who has inflicted a bitter sorrow or injury are similar to the steps for forgiving yourself.

Steps to Forgiving Others

Faith	1. Ask God for courage.
	2. Reflect on the act without rationalizing or editing its import. Tell it to a trusted friend.
Charity	3. Visualize the wrongful party and their suffering, even if they are not remorseful.
	4. Acknowledge the cost to you in maintaining your anger, resentment, and depression.

5. Visualize your relief if you no longer had to pay that cost.

Grace   6. Release your anguish and feel the peace descend upon you. Pray for that party.

Before I end this essay on forgiveness, I want to share a prayer that seems to sum it all up very nicely.

Prayer of St. Francis

Lord, make me an instrument of your peace
where there is hatred, let me sow love;
where there is injury, pardon;
where there is doubt, faith;
where there is despair, hope;
where there is darkness, light;
where there is sadness, joy.

O divine Master, grant that I may not so much seek
to be consoled as to console,
to be understood as to understand,
to be loved as to love.
For it is in giving that we receive,
it is in pardoning that we are pardoned,
it is in dying that we are born to eternal life.
Amen.

Final thoughts . . .

Your sojourn has been an arduous labor. You have learned many things along the way, not just from the written words of the sessions, but more significantly through the actions you have taken. God has allowed us, through free will, to create our own reality—physically, emotionally, and spiritually. God has been our first, and perhaps only, loving parent, who has seen us through challenging times and circumstances. We are each responsible for our actions, but if we forge deep within ourselves and listen to our souls, miracles occur. When we first began, I invited you to establish healing goals to soothe your distress and right your injustices. I spoke with you about how mental illness and physical afflictions were like cancers of the soul but could be overcome through self-understanding and spiritual growth. Your suffering can be replaced with peace, your angst with serenity.

Each session introduced or reminded you of the basic tenets of the process of healing. We addressed meaning, the foundation and central goal of life. Our beliefs were examined in the ways that they help to comprise how we see ourselves. We probed the importance of our family of origin and its impact on our life's course. And, finally, we confronted our fears, our shame, and our ability to forgive.

The central theme that ran gracefully through each session was love. Love is the standard by which all miracles are measured and which ultimately creates our connection with our Creator. Through love we are able to nurture and be nurtured, to give and receive, to protect and be protected. It is only when we depart from love that we create a separateness from God and open the door to the opposite of love—fear. Fear is what illness or disease is all about. Fear is our darkness, a bottomless reservoir of pain. Fear is the thief that robs us of our dignity and our faith and diminishes our soul. Fear prevents us from walking into the light. It is a jealous master that demands our attention and gives the burdens of depression, hopelessness, and, sometimes, death.

Only through love are we liberated to bask in enlightenment and to become peaceful. If we are open, God's gentle whispers will defeat our darkness, and we will feel his grace. Grace will ultimately lead to our redemption from pain and fear.

God bless you.

Appendix

Relaxation Technique

1. First, get nice and comfortable in a quiet place and close your eyes. Take two deep breaths.
2. We will be taking an imaginary trip through your body, and I want you to visualize first your feet. How do they feel? Are they comfortable, do they hurt? Feel the sensation.
3. Next, slowly move up to your legs and become very aware of how they feel. Are your muscles relaxed? Do your legs feel heavy?
4. Now, move up your body and be aware of your back, stomach, shoulders, arms, neck, and face.
5. Now, let's go inside your head and see how it feels in your mind. Does it feel dark, light, heavy? What is going on inside?
6. Now that you have gone from your feet to your head, be aware of any part of your body that is sending you messages. Is there pain or tension anywhere? What is your body telling you?
7. Now, it is time to ask your body how you feel? Ask yourself, what is it like inside of me?
8. Finally, think for just a minute of an uncomfortable situation, something that has upset you. Hold on to it for thirty to forty seconds. Now where are you feeling it? Does it make your head hurt, give you back pain, upset your stomach?

That is your body communicating with your mind and with you! Becoming aware of this communication will help you find the healing you deserve. To really help, however, you ask the Holy Spirit to help you love yourself. My friend Ed Foreman[21] says to have a great day; do special things just for you and begin your day by:

1. Getting up early
2. Reading something inspirational
3. Exercising
4. Eating a good breakfast
5. Planning your workday
6. Maintaining good nutrition throughout the day
7. Making time for some play
8. Meditating

These are wise words and rules and are conducive to happy days.

Do's When Feeling Angry

1. Speak up when an issue is important to you. Obviously we do not need to address personally every irritation that comes along, but it is a mistake to stay silent if something causes us to feel bitter, resentful, or unhappy.
2. Take time out to think about the problem and to clarify your position. Before you speak out, ask yourself the following questions:
   a. What is it about the situation that makes me angry?
   b. What is the real issue here?
   c. Where do I stand?
   d. What do I want to accomplish?
   e. Who is responsible for what?
   f. What, specifically, do I want to change?
   g. What are the things I will and will not do?
3. Speak in "I" language. Practice saying . . .
   I think . . . I feel . . . I am . . . I fear . . . I want. . . .
   A true "I" statement says something about the self without criticizing or blaming the other person and without holding the other person responsible for your feelings or reactions.
4. Try to appreciate the fact that people are different. We move away from fused relationships when we recognize that there are as many ways of seeing the world as there are people in it. If you're fighting

about who has the "truth," you may be missing the point. Different perspectives and ways of reacting do not necessarily mean that one person is right and the other wrong.

5. Recognize that each person is responsible for his or her own behavior. If you are angry about the distance between you and others, it is your responsibility to find a new way to approach the situation.

6. Try to avoid speaking through a third party. If you are angry with someone's behavior, don't say, for example, "I think my daughter felt terrible when you didn't find the time to come to her school play." Instead try, "I was upset when you didn't come. You're important to me, and I really wanted you to be there."[22]

Twelve Rules for Resolving Conflict

1. Carefully consider what is involved in the matter before you turn it into open conflict.

2. Limit the conflict to the present time, that is, to the here and now. Do not use yesterday's problems for today's ammunition. Such common phrases as "you always" and "you never" should be dropped.

3. Keep to one issue. In other words, planning and organization are to be used. It might even be wise prior to the discussion to let the other know that you are going to be talking to him or her about the matter.

4. Use what we call the "I" message. Express your feelings in the first person. The "I" message describes how the speaker is feeling; he expresses his own emotions. The "you" message is a statement of condemnation.

5. Guard against character attack. Do not launch a general attack on the other's personality. Speak in particulars about his behavior.

6. Do not counterattack. Try to accept the statement as an accurate reflection of what he believes to be a problem.

7. Do not attempt to analyze the other person's behavior. Try to analyze your own participation in the problem.

8. Deal with conflicts promptly. The goal is to express your feelings openly and honestly; burying feelings is dishonest.

9. Make sure your emotions are appropriate. The expression of emotions should be proportionate to the size of the conflict.

10. Do not be concerned about winning or losing. The important point is not whether you win or lose, but whether the problem is solved.

11. Determine the limits for your discussion of the conflict. Do not hit below the belt. Comments that are too hurtful or damaging must be avoided (for example, a previous marriage, a recent work failure, and so forth).
12. Establish some method to insure that the rules are followed and to bring about a fair and successful resolution to the conflict. Either person can call "foul" or pull the "stop cord," no matter who started the unfair behavior.[23]

Notes

1. *Diagnostic and Statistical Manual of Mental Disorders,* 3d ed. rev. (Washington, D.C.: American Medical Association, 1987).

2. Abraham H. Maslow, *Toward a Psychology of Being* (New York: Van Nostrand, Reinhold, 1968).

3. Marianne Williamson, *A Return to Love* (New York: HarperCollins, 1992).

4. Marvel Harrison, Ph.D., and Terry Kellogg, CCDP. Coauthors of *Broken Toys, Broken Dreams; Finding Balance; Butterfly Kisses;* and *Reflections,* Harrison and Kellogg are at Life Balance and Life-Works Clinics (505-662-4044).

5. Harrison and Kellogg, Family Rules, seminar handout.

6. Harrison and Kellogg, Healthy Families, seminar handout.

7. Viktor Frankl, *Man's Search for Meaning* (New York: Simon and Schuster, 1962).

8. William Ernest Henley, "Invictus," in *This Singing World,* edited by Louis Untermeyer (New York: Harcourt Brace & Co., 1945).

9. Kent Waldrep and Susan M. Malone, *Fourth and Long* (New York: Crossroad, 1996).

10. Keith Schnert, M.D., *Stress/Unstress* (Minneapolis: Augsburg, 1981).

11. Gary Emery, Ph.D., and James Campbell, M.D., *Rapid Relief from Emotional Distress* (New York: Ballantine Random House, 1987).

12. Lecture by Florence Littauer, Class Speakers Inc., 1645 S. Rancho Sante Fe, Suite 102, San Marcos, CA, 92069.

13. The Gibb categories are from "Defensive Communication," *Journal of Communication* 11/3 (1961): 141–48.

14. Sigmund Freud, *The Complete Psychological Works of Sigmund Freud: Standard Edition* (London: Hogarth Press, 1936).

15. John Bradshaw, *Bradshaw on the Family* (Deerfield Beach, FL: Health Communications, Inc., 1988); and idem, *Healing the Shame that Binds You* (Deerfield Beach, FL: Health Communications, Inc., 1988).

16. C. G. Jung, *Man and His Symbols* (New York: Doubleday, 1964); and idem, *Memories, Dreams, Reflections,* ed. Aniela Jaffee; trans. Richard and Clara Winston (New York: Vintage Books, 1965).

17. Frederick S. Perls, *Gestalt Therapy Verbatim* (Salt Lake City, UT: Real People Press, 1969).

18. Ann Faraday, *The Dream Game* (n.p., 1973).

19. Letter from Kelly to Mary Ellen (1894); by permission. Mary Ellen was the first documented case of child abuse.

20. Dr. O. Carl Simonton, S. Matthews-Simonton, and James Creighton, *Getting Well Again* (Los Angeles: J. P. Tarcher, Inc., 1978).

21. Audio tape "How to Make Every Day a Terrific Day," by Ed Foreman (Dallas: Executive Development Systems, Inc., 1991).

22. Harrison and Kellogg, seminar handout.

23. Harrison and Kellogg, seminar handout.

About the Author

Dr. Ann Patterson Wildemann is a recognized expert in the fields of mental health.

She is an honor graduate of Wright State University, attended the University of Dayton where she received a Master's in Science, and later earned a Ph.D. from Texas Woman's University.

Dr. Wildemann is a clinician in private practice in Arlington, Texas, and is on the staff at Charter Hospital of Grapevine, Texas. She has been a professor in the graduate school at the University of Texas where she broadened her counseling expertise through teaching and research. Today, apart from her private practice, she is an active clinical and business consultant. Dr. Wildemann is the mother of three children and makes her home outside of Dallas.

Many of you are already familiar with "Dr. Ann" because she has been a regular contributor on such national shows as PM Magazine, Hour Magazine, and the CBS network. She has been the host of her own successful television and radio talk shows and is in demand as a speaker and seminar presenter. Through her personal intelligence, warmth, and humor, she has helped many people.

Dr. Ann Wildemann . . . get to know her!